Advance Praise for *The Hidden Stream*

The prelude to *The Hidden Stream* conveys Stephanie Sugioka's intent with forceful grace: "I mean the prose that surrounds these poems to tell of the earth from which the flowers grow. For without this humble stuff of everyday life, there would be no poems." She then invites us "to see how these flowers have come to grow from the raw earth of my being." The interplay of light and shadow, poem and story, of Sugioka's exquisite memoir give access to the inner currents of a life enriched by cultural, spiritual, and intellectual influences, but even more, of a soul attuned to "streams and trees for nurturance and modeling." As she writes in her poem "After Reading *The Tale of Genji*," – " a woman's soul is like wind."

—Suzanne Underwood Rhodes, author of *Flying Yellow*

In her new memoir, Stephanie Sugioka says that hers has been a life that's mostly been "unremarkable." Readers, however, should not let that modest appraisal deter them from following *The Hidden Stream: A Life in Prose and Verse* from its source to where it meets us in the present moment. As graceful as it is honest and heartfelt, her narrative takes readers from her childhood, growing up in "the only Japanese-American (or any sort of Asian) family in the small southern town of Chapel Hill, North Carolina...in the fifties before the civil rights movement;" and then through various relocations and life changes while she reflects on being a daughter, wife, mother, teacher, poet, and writer. The writer asks, "what about the dirt from which these flowers grow . . . roots, worms, and decaying leaves?" The poems included in this memoir fold and uncover,

uncover and fold, with origami-like precision, various moments that reward with their insight, ache, and quiet beauty.

> —Luisa A. Igloria, author of *The Buddha Wonders if She is Having a Mid-Life Crisis* and *Ode to the Heart Smaller than a Pencil Eraser*

In this lovely, thoughtful memoir of poems and prose—a hybrid form whose ancestry is the Japanese *haibun*—the inner world flowers through the poems, while the prose gives them a chronological and autobiographical frame. The work has an eloquent clarity, purity and a genuine modesty; the reader is respected, invited in, drawn into a world where life and art are one, and union becomes communion as we recognize ourselves in the clear and moving mirror of *The Hidden Stream*.

> —Eleanor Wilner, 2019 Frost Medalist and author of *Before Our Eyes: New and Selected Poems 1975-2017*

The Hidden Stream

A Life in Prose and Verse

Stephanie Sugioka

Unicorn Bay Press
2020

The Hidden Stream
A Life in Prose and Verse
Copyright © 2019 Stephanie Sugioka
All rights reserved
Manufactured in the United States of America
ISBN: 978-1-943416-62-2
Cover Design: Judy Mercier

Unicorn Bay Press, an imprint of Blue Moon Plays
1385 Fordham Road, Ste 105-279
Virginia Beach, VA 34764

www.BlueMoonPlays.com

To Eleanor,
who clearly sees what is hidden

Acknowledgments

Thanks are due to the editors of the following publications, in which the poems that are included here originally appeared:

The Beloit Poetry Journal: "After Reading *The Tale of Genji*"
Calyx: "Surroundings" and "A Commuter in Wisconsin"
Festschrift for Elliott Coleman: "Birds"
The Forbidden Stitch: An Asian American Women's Anthology
     (Calyx Books): "Legacy"
The Sow's Ear: "For a Young Son in Autumn," "Marriage,"
     "Father of Waters," "Van Gogh in a Form of
     Limitation"

I am deeply grateful to:

Eleanor Wilner, who taught me as an undergraduate and has mentored me ever since.

Supportive friends and fellow writers, especially Suzanne Rhodes and Judy Mercier, who designed the cover for this book.

Robert Peebles Arthur, without whose support and encouragement this memoir would never have made it into print.

My husband, Jeffrey Richards, and my son and daughter, Aaron and Sarah Richards, for everything.

I find letters from God dropt in the street, and every one is sign'd by God's name,
And I leave them where they are, for I know that wheresoe'er I go,
Others will punctually come for ever and ever.

—Walt Whitman, *Song of Myself*

THE HIDDEN STREAM

Prelude

My motives for writing this book are various. First, I know that even if I were lucky enough to have a book of my poems published, very few people would read it. The retreat of many poets into the obscure corners of academe and the current appetites of the reading public have conspired to keep most people from reading poetry altogether. Also, I am a mongrel—half Japanese and half Caucasian—and thus my book, a hybrid of poetry and prose, will be made in my image. Finally, I think there's some virtue in trying to tell the whole story of how poems come to be. I see each of my poems as being like a flower (or, less charitably, like a weed, but weeds can blossom too). But what about the dirt from which these flowers grow—the roots, worms, and decaying leaves? These surely deserve a mention as well. I mean the prose that surrounds these poems to tell of the earth from which the flowers grow. For without this humble stuff of everyday life, there would be no poems. And I would like to invite you, my readers, to see how these flowers have come to grow from the raw earth of my being.

Writers have, of course, mixed poetry and prose together before, and my attempt is partly inspired by a book written by the Japanese haiku poet Issa, *The Year of My Life*. This book ostensibly records the events of the year 1819, and it intersperses prose with short poems, a form called *haibun* and created by the earlier haiku poet Basho. The little poems in Issa's book remind me of pearls on a necklace held together only tenuously by a string, which is his prose. I have always identified deeply with Issa. He had one of

1

the saddest lives I have ever heard of: His mother died when he was two, and his stepmother hated him so much that he was forced to live most of his life in exile from his native village. He married late in life, and the three children of that marriage all died in infancy; shortly thereafter, his wife died as well. Nevertheless, unlike his famous predecessor Basho, Issa never aimed to renounce the world but rather to embrace it. Here is an example of his poetry:

> Step aside, step aside,
> Little sparrows,
> His lordship, Sir Horse
> Is coming through.

> —trans. Nobuyuki Yuasa

A Buddhist, he was a poet of the small, the overlooked, the insignificant. He is quintessentially Japanese, and he represents an aesthetic and an ethics that are close to my own.

As his translator, Nobuyuki Yuasa, points out, this "account" of Issa's year is actually an "artistic deception [in] that he has woven into the fabric . . . experiences which came from other years . . . if indeed some of them be not pure fiction." Yuasa goes on to say:

> He has departed from the truth to make it truer. This book is a kind of spiritual garland that he has woven to crown his life. Or, speaking less elaborately, we may say that by

2

means of this volume, he has turned his life into a work of art.

And so my motives are similar to Issa's. According to R. H. Blythe, the editor of the four-volume collection *Haiku*, Issa believed that "our art and poetry are to be put into our living." And this is my belief as well.

In twenty-first century America, art is very much a spectator sport. Music, drama, dance, and poetry stand somehow apart from our everyday experience—relegated to theaters, concert halls, and universities. I have always chafed at what seems to me a sort of cultural schizophrenia. I have a deep need to integrate my art with my life, and this impulse is closely related to my need to incorporate the sacred into my everyday existence. A *New Yorker* columnist whose name I've forgotten once commented, "Life is dumber than fiction." Yes, but does it have to be? Can't our art inform our lives so that they are wiser than before? Can't our lives inform our art so that it has direct bearing on what we feel and do here and now? So that it becomes at least as relevant as the evening stock market report or what we're planning to fix for dinner? This book is my small attempt to bring my life and art together. I am hoping that truth and beauty are not so incompatible after all. Keats would have approved, I think, as would Issa.

The frustrated psychology major in me has also contributed to this effort. I am fascinated by the question of how we construct identity in this crazy patchwork quilt of a country. Is identity more like a bulb whose inevitable destiny is to become, say, a daffodil? Or is it like a bird's nest that has been constructed with a bit of this and a bit of that—a little straw here and a little string there? No doubt, as with all such questions, the answer is somewhere between the two. Nonetheless, I—who am half Japanese, about a quarter English, and about a quarter Cherokee, French, Scotch-Irish, and maybe Dutch—continue to be interested in the process by which we become who we are. So I compose myself, and maybe as you read this book, you will see me becoming who I am and gain some insight into your own identity as well. And if I'm really lucky, eventually some psychology or sociology graduate student will include me as a footnote in her dissertation with a title like "Negotiating Identity in a Cross-Cultural Context: A Study of the Effects of Racial and Ethnic Heterogeneity in Twenty-first Century America." I can always hope.

I have never been able to regard writing as anything other than an act of communication, and although it is about me and my life, I hope this book will in some way speak directly to you, my readers. I see myself as a sort of Everywoman: a child of the fifties and sixties, of divorce, of irreconcilable contradictions. I have lived in the Southeast, the Northeast, and the Midwest and spent much of my early life crisscrossing the country to visit my mother and other relatives in California. I have lived a year in Europe and a year in China. Isolated by geography from my Japanese relatives, I have also never really felt at home in Euro-America. I have walked at the edges of so many worlds, yet I belong to none. Do you, my readers, see anything of yourselves in me? Am I as alienated as I suppose? Or are we all misfits in one way or another? All wayfaring strangers wandering through a land that we can never fully belong to, that can never fully belong to us? I hope that what I write here will bring all of us nearer to the answers of these questions. And I hope that you will find some value or pleasure in keeping me company for a while on this journey.

The Hidden Stream

My life has, in most ways, been unremarkable. It has not been marked by cataclysmic events, terrible injuries, or horrific abuses. I have never served in the Peace Corps or studied with a Tibetan lama. Much of my journey has not been visible to the physical eye. It has been an inner journey—a hidden stream. Probably this is true of many people. Their outward lives seem ordinary, and they reveal little of their inner stories, and so when they die, these stories die with them. I do not want this to happen to me. I want to tell my inner story so that, at the very least, my friends and relatives will understand what the events of my life—meager though they may seem from the outside—have meant to me. I want those who know me to understand my life from the inside out. I have heard it said that those who never manage to tell their stories "die with their music still in them." I want to sing my song before I die.

When I was in my early twenties, I had a dream that I still remember. In the dream, it was my "job" to gather shells and smooth stones and to polish them so that they were even more beautiful than before. I think that these stones and shells are the equivalent of Whitman's "letters from God." And I want this book to be such a gathering of rough objects, which I will polish for you as well as I can. Like Whitman, I believe in the innocence of our original nature. The Buddhists call this "beginner's mind" and the Taoists "the uncarved block." I will probably never be a good Christian because at heart I do not believe in original sin. On the other hand, I do believe that we are, as Gerard Manley Hopkins said, "smeared with toil." The overlay of life in the world sullies and entangles us. As a result, I have a deep distrust of humans and all their devices. Most of the human beings in my childhood were untrustworthy or neglectful, and so I turned to nature—to streams and trees—for nurturance and modeling. To this day, I have no love for finely wrought human objects such as jewelry and antiques. The objets d'arts that decorate my tables and shelves tend to be not Fabergé eggs or glass figurines but shells, driftwood, and river rocks.

The Hollow Reed

My friend Suzanne Underwood Rhodes, who attended the Johns Hopkins Writing Seminars with me, once said something that impressed me deeply. She talked about the importance for writers of being "hollowed out by pain"—thus the title of my first group of poems, "The Hollow Reed." The first poem in this group, "Husks," shows my mistrust of words and other human devices— also the deep influence of the Zen aesthetic on my life.

Husks

Before you begin
to read these words
I must warn you
that they are not
the thing itself—
only leavings,
husks,
hollow as cicada shells.

The real thing, it seems,
is always somewhere else.
It's as if you were to pull away,
one at a time,
the petals of a rose.
You see—what is left,
after the last petal is gone—
this is what I wanted to tell you.

In a similar vein, Thomas Merton says, "The real way to study Zen is to penetrate the outer shell and taste the inner kernel which cannot be defined," and he quotes Meister Eckhart, a Christian Zen master if ever there was one:

> The shell must be cracked apart if what is in it is to come out; for if you want the kernel, you must break the shell. And therefore, if you want to discover nature's nakedness, you must destroy its symbols and the farther you get in, the nearer you come to its essence. When you come to the One that gathers all things up into itself, there your soul must stay.

My next poem is also about breaking—a brokenness that in some mysterious way translates into song. My father was a scientist and an agnostic, and when I was a child, I felt myself forbidden to believe in God. I desperately wanted to and grieved deeply that I could not. (We attended a nondenominational Protestant church—but even that only sporadically.) In my teens I discovered the Eastern religions, and since Buddhism and Shinto had been the religions of my ancestors, I felt them to be a sort of birthright. I immersed myself in the study of Eastern religions— especially Taoism and Zen Buddhism. They seemed to me so much more rational than Christianity, and yet this next poem, written when I was a senior in college, is permeated with Christian symbolism. I might have chosen Buddhism as my adoptive religion, but Christianity, it seems, would continue to choose me.

Allegro Con Spirito

No,
my life doesn't
go that way.
Please,
the song doesn't fit.
Try
to wedge it
between the rigid beats.
See
how it shatters
like a fine crystal goblet.
Would you taste the wine
that it held?

I will hand the pieces round
8

like wafers.
Take one in your mouth,
and when it bites into your tongue,
then
you may know me.
Then you may taste my song.

I associated the Buddhist notion of original mind and the Taoist one of the spontaneous way with the innate purity of nature. For example, if you've ever looked closely at even a common bird like a wren with its little upturned tail or a chickadee with its jaunty black cap, you know that birds are perfect.

Birds

Through the thickness
of summer dusk
I've heard the cool fluid
song of the thrush.
Both question and answer
it is
three notes up,
three notes down.
What can I say?

.

The sound that is left
after the bubbles
of pigeon voices
have broken
against the city's
stone
is a circle.

.

A flock   of birds
makes waterfalls
in the air:
arpeggios
of movement.

They fly
from tree to tree
as though in time
to some silent music.

I too would move
to this music
if I knew it,
if my bones were hollow enough
to sing.

The final poem I include here was written quite recently, that is, over twenty-five years after "Birds," and yet the feathered creature continues in some way to have the advantage over the unfeathered one.

Regret

Just off Highway 64 at dusk
as I hurtled by on my metaled way
with all the other rush-hour traffic,
I glimpsed a dark pond
surrounded on three sides by trees
and overhung with vines.
There a great white egret stood
neck arched,
beak poised,
waiting for that flash of silver
in dark water,

10

wings folded white and still
as the pages of all the books
I have never written.

River's Daughter

My childhood was characterized by deep loneliness. Ours was the only Japanese-American (or any sort of Asian) family in the small southern town of Chapel Hill, North Carolina. This was in the fifties before the civil rights movement, and the "white" and "colored" signs on the doors of the bus station restrooms filled me with uneasiness—not only because I knew in my bones that segregation was wrong but because I sensed that the "colored" sign on the one door might just as easily have referred to me and my family. Though I experienced little overt discrimination, the snickers and hastily erased pictures of slanty-eyed Japs on the school chalkboard were enough to convey to me the undesirability of my race.

I am quite literally a product of racial discrimination. My father's father was one of the lucky ones who had advance notice that the Japanese in California would be "detained" if they did not leave before the deadline on May 9, 1942. He sold his considerable landholdings (farmland and fruit orchards) to a neighbor for a few dollars an acre because he assumed that otherwise they would be confiscated. Then he left the state with the caravan of his family in tow. (One aunt, who was left behind in a hospital with pneumonia, and the other who stayed to care for her were "detained" as soon as the first one was well enough to walk to the railway car that would carry them to Amache internment camp.)

11

When my grandfather and his family arrived in Denver, Colorado, a Disciples of Christ (or Christian) minister helped them to get settled into housing there. His daughter, Marilyn Brown, would eventually marry my grandfather's middle son, Kenneth Sugioka, and I would be the first product of that marriage.

After World War II, most of my father's family drifted back to California, but my father kept pushing eastward — to medical school in St. Louis, Missouri, residency in Iowa City, Iowa, and finally to a position of professor of anesthesiology at the University of North Carolina at Chapel Hill. He did not, however, manage to escape the specter of discrimination, which haunted him well into his academic career. He and my mother were turned away from house after house in Iowa City. Finally the writer Paul Engle came to their rescue when he rented them his house while he was away on sabbatical. It was in this house that they were living when I was born on May 22, 1951.

Growing up in Chapel Hill, I was geographically isolated from my extended family — my mother's in Denver and my father's in Los Angeles. My father's father died when I was only a few years old, and my father's mother, whom I nevertheless adored, spoke very little English even after almost fifty years of living in this country. "Good girl, good girl," she would say over and over again during our rare times together. She would hold me in her bony arms, the top of her head barely reaching my chin. I still have one of her silk kimonos, inscribed with her family crest, and a tiny pair of Japanese clogs that look like they might have belonged to a five-year-old child.

I am convinced that my grandmother's refusal to learn English was an expression of her dislike of the whole American enterprise. She belonged to the Japanese aristocracy and had never washed a dish or prepared a meal in her life before my grandfather brought her to this country to be a farmer's wife. It was, of course, a contract marriage but with a different twist. My grandfather had originally contracted to marry her sister, who died in Japan after giving birth to their child. He then returned from America to Japan to get my grandmother, who was honor bound to raise her sister's child. My grandmother's hatred of that child—a girl, ironically named Grace—is legendary. Apparently, my grandmother had been raised in great luxury and might even have been able to attend a university in Japan had she not been abducted to this barbarian country to fulfill a role she detested. She was a hardy soul, however, and proceeded to bear ten children of her own—seven girls and three boys. My father, the middle son, was her uncontested favorite.

Like many second-generation (nisei) children, my father did his best to shed all but a few traces of his Japanese heritage in favor of a purely American persona. Nevertheless, I identified intensely with the Japanese side of my family, and Japanese culture and its ideals permeated my childhood in subtle ways. I adored my seven Japanese-American aunties, who fed me on sushi and sashimi and treated me like a princess on our rare visits to Los Angeles, where most of them lived. The house my father had built for us in Chapel Hill was all wood and glass—a modern rendering of Japanese architecture. My father sometimes made

13

tempura and sukiaki for us and regularly consumed rice with what we children called "stinky" Japanese pickles. I played with Japanese dolls and dressed up in a red flowered kimono for ceremonial occasions. Although my father made no conscious effort to teach me the language or particular traditions, I managed to absorb much that is essential to Japanese culture through my pores.

When I was in my early twenties, I wrote a poem that attempted to integrate bits and pieces of my Japanese heritage into some sort of coherent whole. Clearly this piece of juvenilia is of historical rather than artistic value, but I think that even its awkwardness is revealing; it shows how hard I had to work to construct an identity from the hodgepodge that was my cultural heritage.

Seppuku

(1)   My father is a samurai doctor.
        He has a samurai sword.
Daddy, the case is urgent
and we must operate.
So take your samurai sword, Doctor,
and split me in two like a watermelon.
Daddy, split me in two.

Half will be red inside
like a Celt or an Anglo-Saxon,
the other half red like a a Jap.
And is this pathological?
Of something cerebral
or cardiovascular?

14

Logic will find a way, Doctor,
so let us dissect.

We have the longitudinal sections,
now we make the cross.

The diagnosis is difficult
isn't it, Doctor?
Though so precisely you slice
with your samurai scalpel,
though you section to slivers of microns
with your samurai microtome,
my disease remains as elusive
as my self.

Truly, my dear father
for you I will always be
that subtlest essence
you do not perceive.

And how, without proof of existence,
can treatment be prescribed,
much less a prognosis ventured?
And how do we term this condition—
neuresthenia of the soul
or a clear case of nothingness?

Truly, my dear father,
I am as elusive as my disease.
Perhaps we are the same.

(2)   My family is a crazy tree.
Daddy, you've caused
my grandmother's hands
to fall like dead leaves
in her lap.

So easily did you transplant
from the West Coast to the East,
so well did your children grow
to be American.
I have many questions for her—
all of them in the wrong language.
There is no tide of words
to bear me backwards,
back to the Inland Sea
Where Grandfather Seijiro
often swam
to escape his stepmother's hate
for a while—
out to a tiny green island
between Honshu and Shikoku.

Nor even back
as far as California
when Seijiro brought his wife
and little more than the
strength of a samurai will
to fill an entire valley
with clouds of flowering trees.

It is only lately I've learned
in translation
how, after the railroads,
the goldmines and garlic fields,
those floating islands of blossoms
finally burst into being.

How my grandfather showed
his affinity for the trees
in a rare talent for grafting

16

say onto an apricot tree
branches of peach and cherry.

How Grandma Kameno
would look out the window
to see it bloom
for the third time that spring
and say with a pragmatist's scorn,
"It's another one of your father's
crazy trees."

How in the wind of 1942
he, Kameno
and all ten children
were blown away eastward
like cherry blossoms
to rest at last on the charity
of a Presbyterian minister
whose daughter was to become
your wife—an absentee mother of mine.
How Amatersu
fell from the skies
to enclose lotus-like
the ancestral home
of my grandfather's family
in petals of flame.

How (and let us be plainspoken
now) they died—every one
of those steel-blooded samurais,
his family, yours and mine,
in Hiroshima on August 6, 1945.

How his heart split
like an overripe plum;
how, sick of eating the rotted

fruit of his dream
he died of stomach cancer
before I was born.

(3)   Mother, I never saw you.
Daddy, I dream of broken Japanese dolls.
They not only cry and wet themselves,
they also bleed at the joints.

But somewhere
in the obscurity of my mind
is one uncluttered room,
where in the tokonoma
there sits an earthen vase
filled with blossoms of flowering apricot,
flowering peach and cherry.

Here a samurai lady walks,
her tiny feet tottering in their clogs
like the wobbling notes of the koto.
She settles over her instrument,
her face white as the moon,
her silks rippling around her
like the waves of a red, red sea.

(Yes truly, my dear father
though your dissections have failed to reveal it,
somewhere in me is song.
It is as elusive as
both me and my disease.
Perhaps we all are one.)

And sometimes at night
my blood surges in me
backwards toward some impossible shore

18

where mist billows up from the rocks
where Mother-dragon-mountain
will feed me her fiery milk
and swallow me
whole.

The samurai sword of the poem is not just a figure of speech. It exists, and my father owns it. It is over two hundred years old and has a long, heavy blade that is wickedly sharp. My father inherited it because he is the only son who has a son, and whichever of my three brothers who has a son will inherit it in turn. They are welcome to it; I would not want it in my house. Splitting people in two like watermelons from the crown of the head neatly down to the groin is exactly what the sword was designed to do and no doubt on some occasion did. My Japanese ancestors were a bellicose lot. I have no illusions about this. The atrocities the Japanese committed in China during World War II, for example, were just the culmination of many centuries of barbarism.

Most of what the poem says about my grandfather is true too. He was descended from samurais but was the second son and, true to Japanese custom, inherited virtually nothing as a result. This—along with a stepmother who made his life a misery—was the reason he came to this country. He had nothing to gain by staying in Japan and thus nothing to lose by coming here. And so he came, but his adopted country proved crueler than his stepmother. It almost simultaneously wiped out his family in Japan and deprived him of his hard-earned lands in California. What the poem does not say is that he was an

19

alcoholic—small wonder, I think. This may have been the only sane response to his outrageous circumstances.

My grandfather had something of the artist about him. An excellent cook (my grandmother never did learn to make a decent meal) and a consummate gardener, he apparently really could graft almost any tree onto any other—an art my father says has since been lost. Though my father was often at odds with his father, they shared a love of growing things. My father's gardens never fail to thrive, and he has a gift for flower arranging as well. At any season of the year, his house is always full of flowers. And it has the traditional raised alcove—the tokonoma—that contains the family's sacred objects. In his tokonoma, his most recent arrangement of camellias, dogwood blossoms, or daffodils coexists with the silk-wrapped samurai sword.

From the beginning, I was my father's daughter. He adored me, and I adored him back. Early in my life, my mother retreated behind her bedroom door, and our black maid ran the household in her absence. When my parents were divorced in 1964, custody of my brother and me was granted to my father while my mother got custody of my sister. Shortly thereafter, in 1965, my mother moved to Berkeley California with my sister. In 1990, when I was only 38, she died of cancer. She was conspicuous by her absence, and I have spent much of my life trying to fill in the great blank spaces that she left behind.

Every woman raised by a father must, I think, find negotiating her identity a tricky business—especially when she is also suffering from a certain amount of cross-cultural confusion, which I was. These next three poems show my attempt during my later twenties and beyond to create myself in a recognizable image. When I read *The Tale of Genji*, it completely captured my imagination because it seemed to provide some tantalizing clues to my identity. And, of course, it was written by a woman—Lady Murasaki—around 1000 A.D. (It was—perhaps arguably—the first novel ever written, and yet I found that, until recently, few Western scholars even knew of its existence.)

After Reading *The Tale of Genji*

In ancient Japan the ladies
draped their souls out of the windows
in silks of acacia yellow, plum blossom red,
wisteria blue, and the ivory of chrysanthemums
that have faded to perfection.
The ladies themselves were hidden
behind blinds, behind screens, behind fans.
And when the silks were folded into their boxes
it was impossible to know
which soul belonged to which woman.

For a woman's soul is like wind
and may only be known by
what it touches
(and so you see I lied—
it was not their souls at all
but only wind-rippled silk).
The men riding by on their horses
were, however, impressed.

In ancient Japan a sword was judged
by how precisely it might sever a flower
without disturbing the plant
from which the flower came.

Once there was a river with no bridge.
On one side, screened by bamboo,
there walked a lady with a flower,
on the other a man with a sword.
But his horse would not cross the water
and disgusted he threw his sword into the river.
For a woman's soul is like water.
It is futile to try to slice it
with even the finest of swords.

In ancient Japan the man
would throw the image of his beloved
into the river
hoping the gods would find it
and deliver her to him.
But the water would wear the image smooth
by the time it had reached the gods
and so the gods were confused
as to who was the beloved.

At the bottom of the river
a sword lies rusting
and over the river the willows hang
like grieving ladies-in-waiting.
For a woman's soul is like water
and may only be known
by a drowning.

The woman in this poem constantly eludes the man. As fluid as water, as mercurial as wind, she slips away from his grasp as he tries to define her with steel or stone.

In my late twenties, when I wrote this poem, I had been involved with a number of men, and in all my relationships I suffered from the confusion that had resulted from my odd, inverted relationship with my father. As I said earlier, when he and my mother separated in 1964, my sister stayed with my mother, and my brother and I went with my father. My father, brother, and I lived in a series of houses temporarily vacated by university professors on sabbatical. My brother was very withdrawn and my father very depressed. Though we always had a maid to do the laundry and other housework, I became, in some real sense, the mistress of the household. I was the hostess when my father, who was chairman of his department, entertained guests in our home, and I struggled desperately to mediate between him and my brother, who seemed to be in constant conflict. My brother was eleven; I was thirteen. I imagined that I had to be perfect in order to keep the foundering vessel of our family afloat. To do this, I had to meet two sets of expectations that were essentially mutually exclusive: I had to be both the submissive Japanese daughter, the perfect instrument of my father's will, and the successful American daughter, the self-sufficient individual in total control of her life. I had to play the piano like a concert pianist, make straight As in school, and bake a perfect apple pie. Much of this pressure to excel came from my father, but even that could not come close to the pressure I myself created in the crucible that was my thirteen-year-old psyche. I was my father's favorite child, and all I had to do to remain worthy of that honor was to be perfect in all ways at all times.

I wrote this next poem much later in my life, but I think it still reflects my struggle to be both my father's daughter and my own person.

Daphne

I was born of water,
my hair streaming back in waves,
my white robe whipping around me
like a sail.

How could I have loved Apollo?
It was my nature to flee
as it was his to pursue.
How can the deer love the hunter?

And if he had truly loved me,
he would never have wanted to pin me to the ground,
to fix me in his amber regard,
to paw me with his claws of stone.
If he had really loved me,
he would have let me go.

I felt his hot breath on my neck
rank as the maw of a ravenous dog.
So I called to my father the river,
thinking he'd sweep me to safety.
But my blood seemed to stop within me.
And as I felt my limbs stiffen,
I thought that Apollo had won.

24

I was to be his tree,
my boughs a sign of his triumph—
but only in the eyes of the world,
that medusa of false vision.

Underneath my bark
my sap still ran.
I abandoned my limbs to the wind.
The living water flowed into my roots
and up to my outermost branches.

I called to the creatures of river and wood,
and my words became tender new leaves.
Deer came to nibble them
and rabbits to sleep in their shade.
A small bird sang in my branches,
his song so high and clear it pierced my heart.

At first glance, it might seem odd that I should identify with the river rather than the sea. Rivers are few and far between in the North Carolina Piedmont where I grew up. And during my early childhood, we always spent summer vacations at the beach on Ocracoke Island, off of Carolina's Outer Banks. At that time, there was no bridge or ferry boat to the island, so we'd cross the sound in a mail boat. We stayed at Miss Bessie's boardinghouse (there were no hotels yet) in sunny wall-papered rooms, where we ate her delicious home-cooked meals. Because the island lacked a clinic or even a physician, the islanders came to my father for treatment during our visits. And the local land baron, Sam Jones, entertained us sumptuously at his palace-like estate. Thus we were made to feel a little like visiting royalty. My brother and I spent most of our time digging with our plastic shovels for Blackbeard's treasure (rumored to be buried there), which we were absolutely sure we would unearth at any moment. We caught buckets of flounder and blue fish in the surf and ran wild as the ponies we sometimes saw across the wide expanses of sand between the dunes and the sea.

But among all these delights, I was never really happy. The tension between my parents hung between me and my surroundings like a choking fog. And I can remember thinking when I was six years old that I was terribly depressed, that I was far too young to be depressed, and that, further, I was too young to know that I was too young to be depressed. Life seemed utterly devoid of meaning. For a six-year-old, happiness and meaning are almost synonymous.

And so the ocean, as much as I loved it, had become associated for me with my mother and her problems. (My mother did, in fact, especially love the sea, and when she died, her ashes were, in accord with her wishes, scattered over the Pacific Ocean.) My parents' separation marked an end to the beach vacations that had been such an important part of my childhood, and in the summer of 1965, my father, brother, and I headed westward to the North Carolina mountains instead.

Our destination was the Celo Valley in the Blue Ridge Mountains, where my father intended to buy a few acres of land for a summer home. During this initial trip we stayed in rustic cabins on the grounds of a nearby private school, sleeping on rough-hewn bunks between sheets and blankets saturated with the wet mountain air. My brother Colin and I were instantly taken with the beauty of the place and excited at the prospect of owning land there. We had been living in a succession of houses belonging to strangers, but this mountain property would truly be ours. The lush greenery—oaks, hemlocks, rhododendrons, ferns, and moss—surrounded and cradled us. The property my father bought bordered a small river—the South Toe—which ran clear over smooth rocks and then deepened into dark green pools. The air smelled of clean water, lush vegetation, and decaying leaves—the headiest smell I've ever known. Halfway up the hillside was the house—a shack really—with no indoor plumbing except the kitchen faucet, where ice cold water came from a spring further up the mountain.

The house faced west, where some of the tallest mountains in Appalachia rear up to form a ridge whose colors change constantly over the course of the day. At midmorning, each tree on the ridge is clear and distinct, but by afternoon the mountains turn a hazy blue. In the evening they grow darker and darker until they finally merge with the blackness of the night. Very early in the morning, the ridge is often covered with fog, which the sun gradually burns away. Watching the mountains emerge from the fog is like seeing the world created anew each morning. It was in the place that I had the first inkling of who exactly I might be. This is the subject of my next poem.

Surroundings

To the one who overcomes . . . I will give a white
stone, and on it a new name written, which no one
knows but the one who receives it.
                            —Revelation 2:17

Here where the shapes of the mountains
are vague enough to form the body of night
I am almost contained.
The wood of the swinging bridge
is the fragile splintered silver of bone.
Beneath, the river rushes
in this deep vein of the mountains.

On either side of the path to the cabin
the cricket voices rise and fall—
bright bits of sound
in two great gourds
that shake as if in answer
to one another.
The quaver of the screech owl's call
is a tin cup filling slowly
with black water.
By the dingy lamplight of the cabin
the strands of my work are almost golden.
With my hook I catch the thread
joining each stitch to the other
forming an open, a spiderweb, pattern—
an exercise in containing emptiness.
Or, if you will, I've left places
for the dark ragged breath of God
to blow through.

There are spaces also in my body
that I feel as I lie in the mildewed bed.
I am waiting for a word.
Perhaps it will be a name.
It will be as silent as
the O of a fish's mouth.
It will be a white stone
dropping quickly
through dark water.

Ghosts

My early life was characterized by absence—the absence of God (seemingly), the absence of a mother, the absence of a home, and, finally, the absence of a family. To do her justice, my mother, I think, took good care of me when I was an infant. She seemed to enjoy feeding me, cuddling me, playing with me, and dressing me in my little bonnets and pinafores. However, after my brother was born in December 1952—only a year and a half after I was—she lapsed into a severe postpartum depression, from which I'm not sure she ever fully recovered. Some of my earliest memories are of her going into her bedroom, shutting the door, and not emerging for the entire day. After our maid left in the evening, we children ran wild. We would start rummaging through the cupboards for food—peanut butter, cereal, anything we could find. Finally at 8 o'clock or later, my father would come home in his blood-stained labcoat, exhausted from having worked in the operating room since 5 a.m. and dismayed to find us children wild-eyed with hunger and our mother still closeted in her bedroom. It was not a pretty sight. Then the fighting would begin, my father accusing my mother of neglecting us, my mother countering that she had no intention of fixing dinner if he came home too late to eat it with us.

One of the few things my parents had in common was a certain lack of restraint. We children would retreat to our bedrooms and bury our heads under pillows to block out the shouting. During one of these fights, my mother hurled half a set of dishes against the kitchen wall. When I was a few years older, I would hear from my mother that my father had tried to push her down the stairs and from my father that she had tried to run him over with the car. To this day, I have no idea how much substance there was to any of these accusations. And then I knew only that whatever was wrong between my parents was too bad to be fixed. When I was eight or nine, I was already wondering why they hadn't separated (though I understand that most children want their parents to stay together at all costs). In those days, psychiatry was in its infancy. My parents did see a therapist for a time but to no good effect apparently. And shortly after I turned thirteen, in the summer of 1964, they separated for good.

One bright spot in our lives had been the election of John F. Kennedy in 1960. We were ardent supporters and regarded Richard Nixon as the archvillain of politics. Kennedy was, of course, assassinated in 1963, the year of the final disintegration of my parents' marriage. I have always associated his death with the dissolution of my life as I had known it. I was sitting in my seventh-grade English classroom when the class cutup came into the room and said in an offhand manner that the president had been shot. No one believed him. A few minutes later the official word came over the intercom system, and I still didn't believe it. I had been raised on Westerns—*Maverick*, *Gunsmoke*, and *Bonanza*—where the hero always shot the bad guy, not the other way around. But when classes were suspended so that we could watch every grim black-and-white minute of the funeral on television, I had to accept that the good guy was dead. And God, as far as I knew, had already died a long time ago. In the space of a year, my private and public worlds were shattered, and I have been trying to put the pieces back together ever since.

In 1965, during the same summer that my father brought our Blue Ridge Mountain property, my mother moved with my sister to Berkeley, California. I regretted not so much her departure as that of my sister Kimi, who was only seven years old at the time. Born when I was seven, Kimi had been my pet; I had cuddled her, changed her diapers, and played with her. She had been the one person in my life on whom I'd thought it safe to lavish my affection unreservedly, and now she was gone.

A year later, in the summer of 1966, my father remarried. His new wife, Mary, had previously been his lab assistant. She was twenty-eight; he was forty-six. My new stepmother was only thirteen years older than I. Two months after the wedding, my brother and I went to boarding school—he to Groton School in Connecticut, I to the North Carolina School of the Arts in Winston-Salem, where I had been accepted to study drama. After that, my brother and I never spent more than a summer at a time with my father and his wife. In the space of a year, I had in some

31

sense lost my mother, my sister, my father, my brother, and my home.

In 1968, my father and stepmother built a beautiful architect-designed house in the woods south of Chapel Hill proper and had their first child, a son named Nathan. It was perfectly clear to my brother and me that they were beginning a new life in which we had no real place. My whole life took on an air of insubstantiality, of unreality, in which people and things were characterized by their absence. Thus this next poem, which I wrote when I was in my early twenties:

Legacy

This is the eldest daughter
of wind and of wood.
Her words are as irrelevant
and as lost
as the broken song
of wind and bamboo.
The boys,
only three and five,
are unaware that I
am a species of ghost
in this their high glass house.
(The older one still insists
his mother must be mine.)
So when I arrive
they run figure eights around me,
triumphantly announcing
that I am there
(and, gullible as always,
I believe them.)

This is the eldest daughter.
A small sound gnaws at her sleep,
a tedious, uneasy creaking
of pine branches
crossed
against one another.
Today, for some reason,
my father and stepmother
want to discuss their wills.
It is understood that the boys
should inherit the house.
Of an oriental design,
made to let in as much light
as the dogwoods, maples, and oaks
will allow,
it manages, somehow,
to look like an airport.
This is the house
that sprang phoenix-like
from the ruins of the former,
(my other) family.
(I've never lived there myself.)
      This is the eldest daughter.
      Music pierces her skull
      like twirling needles.
      It is the Japanese flutes
      that sing the panicked movement
      of her hands
      like broken-winged birds.
We finish our discussion
with a wicked stepmother joke,
and I take my leave.
Then out with the boys
to the rock garden
to learn who has watered
which crocus.

And they shall inherit
a house of light.
I believe in their small round lives
as I believe
in the round white stones
at our feet.

> This is the eldest daughter
> of wind and of wood.
> Her legacy is a house
> where no light shines.
> The reeds sing it
> whispery lullabies,
> and hemlocks stroke
> its splintered sides.
> She is the black wind
> that haunts the house—
> rushing, always rushing
> out of the room
> down the hall
> around the corner
> to find the mother
> to find the father
> who do not own the house
> who are not there.

And so my world was a broken place—forsaken by the God I had never permitted myself to believe in. But still, I couldn't help hoping for and looking for a redeemer—someone to put the world back together again. And, like so many women before me, I looked for that redeemer in a man. When I was twenty-four, I almost married a man I had been dating for some seven years. He was kind, attractive, and intelligent. He was attending medical school, just as I had planned that he would. But I was haunted by the feeling that there was something missing, that somehow I needed more. So I canceled the wedding at the last moment, and not long thereafter I started dating another man. My new love was also attractive and intelligent—intensely so—but he was also less stable and predictable. There was an edge to him, and our relationship was problematic from the first. Looking back, I think that I might well have settled for my first love if I had not been looking for God in all the wrong places.

This next poem attempts to answer the question of the title: What is left after the things that ordinarily make us human have been stripped away? It is about a quest for the divine being that I wasn't at all sure existed but was compelled to seek nevertheless.

What Is Left

I am one who follows the first-born of the dead.
I call his name—he will not answer.
I call his many names.
He walks, receding quickly, and will not turn his head.
He blends with the leaves of the trees and is gone
like a fish into shadowy water.

I have pried behind the blind eye
for the blind man has all of darkness
as the deaf-mute does all of silence
and only the handless man may reach God.

What is left after the world has broken
the pieces like bright glass jangling
in the cold eye of the sun?

What is left after the leaves have fallen,
their colors already fading
out of mind?
(The wind is shuffling through them

like a survivor through old papers
anxiously seeking a message or a sign.)

What is it that waits between our words,
breathes between our breaths?
Who waits just outside of the light of our lamps
like silence
to speak?

I bring you offerings of food.
See how meekly the carrot
lies on the plate.
And you will cut the meat.
You will chop the wood.
The sticks will crack
in your supple, long-fingered hands.
How gently you lay the logs on the grate
to make a cradle of flame.

And after you've lain in the place
that was hewn for you before time,
after the bed is split and I lie broken,
whose body is left
to hold the world together?

Now it is winter when things
draw back into themselves.
I wait in all the spaces between.

You could almost be he.
I look for your face in crowds

where I know you can't be.
Wherever I look it is you
who are missing.

Him I cannot see because
he is everywhere I look.
He is not only the rock
but where the rock is split.
He is the blind wound waiting,
the mute mouth calling.
I am absorbed into him like light.
I have seen behind the blind eye
a planet made almost new—
a naked girlchild running
through green transparent as fire.

She is calling my name.
She is calling my many names.
I reach for her with my handless arms.
She is coming, always, closer.
Now she is almost here.

I'm not at all sure I knew what I was trying to say when I wrote this poem, but I am struck, when I read over it now, by how close in spirit it is to some of the ideas propounded in the writings and the writings and sermons of Meister Eckhart, the thirteenth- to fourteenth-century mystic, whom, however, I had not yet read when I wrote the poem. Simply put, he believed that poverty of the spirit was the ultimate virtue because only by emptying oneself of all possessions and all other preoccupations could the individual make room for the divine. In this way, the mystic prepares him or herself for divine union—which, finally, however, can happen only by virtue of God's grace. The result of this divine union, according the Eckhart, is the divine birth—an internal event that then recurs perpetually in the core of the human soul.

I had not read Eckhart, but I had read T.S. Eliot, who was (and maybe still is) one of my favorite poets. And Eliot refers frequently in his poems to St. John of the Cross's dark night of the soul, which is similar in nature to Eckhart's poverty of the spirit. And, of course, I had also read much about Zen Buddhism, and several thinkers—Thomas Merton and Daisetz Suzuki among them—have pointed out the similarity between Eckhart's emphasis on self-empying and the Zen virtue of detachment. So clearly, I had encountered these ideas before. Even so, my thinking seems closest to Eckhart's, whose works, as I said, I had I had not yet read.

And all of this was, of course, a result of my theological groping—my attempt to fill the vacuum of my religious education. I have come, however, to see this not as a deprivation but as an advantage. My lack of religious training has allowed me to come to Christianity with very few preconceptions. I am free, for example, to think of the holy ghost as female rather than male.

The Holy Ghost

She is the ghost of a virgin.
Silent as dusty sunlight
she enters
and gathers around her the sisters
with their almost invisible lives.

(Thin the wedding veil
wrapped in tissue paper
lying at the bottom
of the cedar chest,

38

thin the photographs
pasted on black pages
of grandchildren's children
in distant places.
Fragile the china
locked in dusty cupboards,
fragile the bones
wrapped in weary flesh.)

In the sunlit Sunday school room
the elder church ladies gather
for coffee cake and prayers.
Discreetly cups clink on saucers.
Their murmured "Our Father"
is dry leaves falling.
"Happy Birthday to you," they sing
in voices faded as ancient flowers
pressed inside yellowed Bibles.
One by one they go.
And yet one by one they return—
gathering in the silences
as dust seems to gather in sunlight.

Having covered the ghostliness of father, mother, home lover, church, and God, I come to possibly the ghostliest of them all: words. I wish I could say with Dylan Thomas that I have a love affair with words, but the truth is that I am profoundly ambivalent toward them. We have, on a good day, a sort of love-hate relationship. In my reading about Western and Eastern mysticism, I've noticed a split that parallels my thinking on this subject. In the Christian tradition, the word is, of course, potentially an embodiment of the divine: "In the beginning was the word, and the word was with God, and the word was God."

Christ is "the word made flesh," and only the sacred words of the Bible can authenticate Christian experience.

Eastern traditions, on the other hand, do not, on the whole, see words as a means to salvation; in fact, as with Zen Buddhism or Taoism, words are more likely to be regarded as obstacles to enlightenment or the Tao. (There have been, however, notable exceptions such as certain popular Buddhist sects in China that made extravagant claims for the miraculous power of the Buddha's name.) Where the aim is the direct experience of the ultimate reality, words come between the seeker and the thing itself. Thus to a question such as, "What is the Buddha?" the Zen adept T'ung-shan replied, "Three pounds of flax." His point, of course, was that words are wholly inadequate to the task of communicating anything about the Buddha. As the *Tao Te Ching* says, "The way that can be named is not the eternal way." And so the Zen/Taoist ideal is a state of wordlessness—or more accurately, a wordless awareness.

I often find myself longing for such a state. I do not watch talk shows on television or listen to radio news. Although I teach, I do not particularly even like to hear myself speak and so find myself on the listening end of most conversations. And sometimes when our Presbyterian minister's sermon lasts for more than fifteen minutes, I feel flayed and overwhelmed and begin half-seriously to contemplate becoming a Quaker instead. What stops me, of course, is that at a Friends meeting, there would be no music, and I cannot do without song.

40

On the other hand, I must confess that words have, in so many ways, been my salvation—and not just Frost's "momentary stay against confusion." In spite of what the Zen Buddhists may say, experience is slippery stuff, and words are the only means I know of wrestling it into coherence. When I was twenty-six, I began keeping a journal, and in that journal I have worked out my salvation—such as it is. It is probably a fascination with words that led me to my quixotic study of the Chinese language. I think I imagined that learning the characters (all forty-seven some thousand of them), or words-as-pictures as I thought of them, might allow me to decode the very secret of human existence. I am sorry to report that this is not what happened, but I still find the characters beautiful and evocative—a tantalizing hint of the word made flesh.

What I tell my students about the words in the works of literature they read is that they are like Koolaid or instant coffee—useless and meaningless until people add to them the water of their attention and experience. Words sitting in dusty tomes on library shelves are dead. We breathe them into life by speaking and reading them, by thinking and writing about them. This is the process by which the word is made flesh. I also tell my students that they will have life more abundantly if they read literature. Someone once said that reading poems and stories adds to the reader's "available store of reality," and someone else that writing literature allows the writer to have a "life within a life." To me, it seems almost miraculous that all this is possible by means of these flimsy little symbols called words.

Writing words is physically uncomfortable for me, and my handwriting is notoriously bad, so I am as dependent on a computer as everyone else. However, also like everyone else, I am much more pleased to find a real letter in my mailbox-the heavy paper inscribed with a curvaceous handwritten message—than to see the little box on my computer screen that says I've "got mail." The paper—that slender sheet of tree—is the flesh, the ink the blood. The words on the computer screen seem ghostly and unsubstantial by comparison.

Word Processing

The computer has swallowed my poems,
sucked the white words
into the vast black hole
of the screen.
And when the printer spews them back out
all that is left are random black marks
on the paper.

No, I say,
That is not what I meant at all.
These things are all flat and black.
My poems have color and weight.
In them people speak and move,
suns rise and rivers flow.

Look, lady, growls the printer.
I'm just doing my job.

And so, you might ask, during my first twenty-five years or so, did anything in my life seem solid and reliable, i.e., *not* ghostly? And I would have to answer no, not really. I was sure of only one thing: that rivers and trees were much more trustworthy than people and words. My life was oddly blank and my sense of self, as a result, almost nonexistent. My greatest fear was that I too might be a ghost—that like the vampires in the Dracula movies of old, I might one day look in the mirror to find no one there at all.

Watercolors

When I look back on the fifty some years I have lived, I tend to see the first twenty-five or so in black and white. It is as if color seeped into my life only gradually, rather as it did in the movie *Pleasantville*. (And this comparison is apt for more than one reason: I was raised in the fifties, when much of the action of the movie takes place.) I think of my real life as beginning only after my marriage in 1978.

In the fall of 1975, I was back in Chapel Hill after a year in Baltimore and a Master's degree in the Writing Seminars from Johns Hopkins. I began working on the editorial board of the literary magazine the *Carolina Quarterly*, the main editor of which was an English graduate student named Jeffrey Hamilton Richards. The *Quarterly* office was small and narrow, no larger than a walk-in closet. I kept (literally) bumping into the editor, who I assumed regarded me more as a physical obstacle than a human being. But one day he surprised me by asking me out to lunch at the Carolina Coffee Shop on Franklin Street in Chapel Hill. Over lunch, we talked nonstop for two hours. And that was the beginning of the relationship that would culminate in our marriage in 1978.

A year after we were married in Chapel Hill, we moved to Wisconsin, where I had been accepted to study Chinese literature

43

at the University of Wisconsin in Madison and where Jeffrey had a job teaching at a small college—Lakeland—near Sheboygan. Between the year of our move in 1979 and the one in which I completed my degree in 1982, I commuted the hundred or so miles between the two towns almost every week. The poem that follows is about that commute, but it is also about my marriage:

A Commuter in Wisconsin

Blue is the color of distance.

—Tennessee Williams, *Camino Real*

Here the land is loud.
Like a litany the lakes
repeat the refrain of sky.
The wind strums the grasses
and the corn speaks in tongues.
Honeysuckle embalmed
the place from where we'd come.
There anything could hide beyond a hill.
Here the land is almost flat:
there's no use denying a thing.

The roads after their crossings
stretch like arms
bared to the sky.
Oh, Lord, we have traveled
in the asphalt of your wounds.

In August when we came
pale blue flowers grew all along the roadside
(but no one seemed to know their name).
They squinted up at the glare of sky
like pious, near-sighted young men.

Quickly the land goes stark
like a charcoal drawing
until sunset when a bruise of color
spreads across the horizon.

The corn mutters dryly to itself
the road stretching like a tongue to water.
Raw the earth with fields
plowed into its sides
screams up black at the sky
until the snow responds with its mute white answer.

And now the green awakening—
the burst of wide-eyed rose
and shy anemone unfolding along the roadside,
again the grasses billowing their hymn.

Your arms like roads reaching toward me
shimmer with a promise of distance.
I am the one who is leaving
and the one who is coming home.

I completed the work for my Master's degree in the spring of 1982, when I was also expecting my first child. When I was eight months pregnant, I took and passed the rather grueling exams that would allow me to get my degree. As it happened, the birth of my son, Aaron, and the granting of my degree took place almost simultaneously: the date on my certificate is May 23, and my son was born on May 24 (two days after my birthday on May 22). Up to that point, I had had an apartment and at least a modest social life in Madison. But after my son was born, I suddenly found myself stranded in a small working-class town with no car and virtually no friends. By this time, my husband had become chair of his department in addition to teaching five courses a semester. He left home early and returned late every day. Virtually my only contact with another adult was the occasional exchange of pleasantries with my landlord or landlady. I loved caring for my little son, but I was desperately lonely.

It had been three years since we'd moved from the Southeast, and not only did I find myself missing family and friends there, but, perhaps even more, I missed the place itself. I missed mockingbirds and mourning doves, dogwoods and redbuds, the Atlantic Ocean and the Blue Ridge Mountains. I had always thought of my life as a series of exiles beginning with my grandfather's exile from Japan, which, as I've said earlier, resulted from the meagerness of his inheritance and the hatred of his stepmother. The next exile was the one suffered by my grandfather and father when the Japanese Americans were forced to leave California during World War II. For me, the ultimate result of this was my isolation from my Japanese relatives, most of whom moved back to California while my father moved further eastward. And this sense of isolation was intensified when, ironically, my mother took my sister and moved out to California after my parents were divorced. So when I found myself, as I perceived it, stranded between the two Coasts, I interpreted this as yet another exile in a series. I chafed and agonized and plotted ways we might move back to the Southeast. No doubt, if I had had a stable family background and a solid marriage, I would have felt differently. But, with respect to parenting skills, my mother was useful to me only as a negative example, and my

46

marriage was shaky. It had never been rock solid, but as the years went by, Jeffrey seemed to become more distant as I became more resentful.

The net result of all of this was that I came to think of myself as being absolutely alone—except, that is, for the company of my baby son. Often it felt to me as if we were truly the only two people in the world. Fortunately, mothering came naturally to me, and I enjoyed nursing him, bathing him, dressing him, playing with him, and reading to him. (He was a literary baby, perhaps as a result of my having read the complete works of Anthony Trollope while I was nursing him, and from infancy, he would sit on my lap and allow himself to be read to for as long as my voice and patience held out.)

My life was reduced to the basics: I baked bread, made soup, washed diapers, and nursed my son. The bitter cold and heavy snow kept us indoors much of the time from November until April, but whenever the weather permitted, I would walk him in his stroller all around our rather pretty little town.

For a Young Son in Autumn

In a reverie we drifted
through your first autumn
like leaves down the river
that runs through our picturebook town:

The park—
its prim white bandshell,
birches and maples
arching to take us in.

The river floating through clouds
of dreamy willows
where goldfinches flit
like chips of errant sunlight.

The town cemetery
where we visit the gentle dead,
as slowly we walk through their slow autumn dream,
while among the spruce and pine
the blue jays split the air
with their prophetic cries.

The road
that leads up the hill
between two churches,
at the top the rows of houses
ending abruptly—
woods on one side,
cornfields on the other.
We turn around and the town
spreads out below us—
toy houses, factories, and stores—
all, my son, for you.

It was fall and we were rich.
The trees with infinite grace
gave up their leaves
and we wallowed in their wealth.

Already for me these images tend
to run together like watercolors,
and for you they'll be like dreams forgotten on waking.
But I want to keep the pages
of this your first picturebook
crisp as autumn leaves,

their colors as sharp as your laughter
in the chill and crystalline air.

On these walks, we would often pass a little white Congregational church a few blocks from our apartment. Only extreme loneliness could have compelled me, who had never regularly attended church in my life, to attend First United Church of Christ in Plymouth, Wisconsin. Thus, as is so typical, in a moment of isolation and desperation, I began my journey toward God.

When the position of church secretary opened up at our little church, I decided it would provide the extra income and social contact that I needed. And so I began working in the quiet, sunny office at the back of the church. It was not quite the life I had envisioned for myself after getting my second Master's degree, but it probably resulted in my spending more hours in church during the few months I worked there than I had during my previous thirty odd years. And it provided the inspiration for the poem "The Holy Ghost," which appears in the previous chapter.

I have tended to think of the six years we spent Wisconsin as the sere season of my life, but when we went back recently for a visit, I was struck anew by the stark beauty of the landscape. It was early April, and there were no leaves on the trees—just dried corn stubble, black earth, and bare branches, with the occasional barn or farmhouse dotting the landscape. And I understood clearly that those years in that particular place were absolutely necessary to my spiritual growth. Kathleen Norris in her book

Dakota exactly describes how such a minimalist landscape allows so perfectly for the blossoming of the soul. Wisconsin turns out not to be such godforsaken country after all.

And it was, after all, the birthplace of my son and inseparable in my mind from his childhood. As Dylan Thomas says in his poem "Fern Hill," "Time allows/ In all his tuneful turning so few and such morning songs/ Before the children green and golden/ Follow him out of grace":

Second Summer

The doctor reached into dripping dark
and plucked out a handful of light.

Son, you burn through my days—
the glittering minutes fly like sparks.
As you run through the house, the light
scatters like confetti.

At night by your bed
I switch on the lamp.
Golden, your hair curls
richly about your head.
I become lost in its intricacies
and do not want to be found.
At the store I cup in my hand a plum
and think of your head—how perfectly round,
of your apple cheek pressed fresh and firm
next to mine.

In our small house the sunlight is humming
the quiet hymn of your sleep.

Wind of a late afternoon
blows from across the fields,
moving over the pond,
lightly touching the willow fronds as it passes.

Heavy with its own weight
your head drops
for an instant on my lap.
Here is no simple light,
but instead the darkness of seeds:
the star at the apple's core.

Autumn has come round again,
and your hair is turning to brown with the leaves.
Yet even now at the touch of the windfall light
its strands glow golden once more.
Thus does the sun pluck its own.

You might be wondering why I've chosen to talk about my
relationship with my son before I have gone into much detail
about the one I had with his father. And the answer is, of course,
that the former was blissfully simple whereas the latter was,
inevitably, a tangled web. And I have no intention of trying to
untangle it here. This would be (1) impossible and (2) boring.
Suffice it to say that our marriage was an unlikely union. He came
from a conservative middle-class family and was raised in the
northern Midwest. I came from a liberal professional family and
was raised in the Southeast. He was a WASP, I was a Japanese
American. He was studying American literature, I Asian. I was
expressive, he reserved. The list of opposites could go on ad
nauseum. But even more daunting than our differences were our
similarities: We were both, for example, perfectionistic firstborn
children with rigid notions of right and wrong and very exacting

expectations of others. All of this should suffice to explain why our relationship during its first fifteen years or so never did run smooth.

My seventeen-year-old daughter was shocked, recently, to learn that our marriage had not always been harmonious, that we had actually had to resort to therapy now and then to salvage it. On the contrary, we constructed it one straw at a time, as a bird does its nest, and only after some twenty-five years can we be reasonably certain that it will weather whatever storms may come its way. But in some crazy way, it does seem to work. Somehow, misfits that we were, we managed to make the world possible for each other, as this poem attempts to convey.

Marriage

Always the first one up
to brew the coffee
you make the darkness clear.
As you call to me your voice
is sunlight through shadowy water.

You are my blue heron husband.
With my water body I lap at your legs.
My wind fingers touch the feathers
about your bony head.

Already with your waking movements
you've woven a white net of morning
to scoop me safe from sleep.

From the musk melon vines you grew in summer,
the shivering line of geese in flight,
the bright bits of Christmas ribbon, pine needles, and twine,

we have woven a garment of seams
the between us we will wear lightly
all the rest of our lives.

Closely we wrap round ourselves
the green hills of Wisconsin.
And at night we smolder softly,
folding into each other
as in wings.

Ours was by no means the perfect marriage, and I was far from being a perfect mother, but in some way my new family gave me a real chance to start over after the botched beginning of the family I was born into. Unlike my mother, I never suffered from post-partum depression, and in fact when my daughter was born in 1987, I felt as if I were experiencing postpartum euphoria instead. For the first several months after her birth, I felt very powerful and alive; this may all have been the result of a fluctuating hormone levels, but it felt real enough.

A great delight of my daughter Sarah's childhood for me was discovering how much her own person she was even at a very young age. We are so unlike that her very existence seems almost miraculous to me. For one thing, where sounds are almost everything to me, she is intensely visual. And this was clear as early as her third year, when she began to produce the pictures I describe in the next poem.

The World According to Sarah Grace

When the whole world goes gray
and I find myself waiting
in flat expanses

blank as Antarctica on the globe
for some sign of life,
I take out Sarah's art.

"Come on," says the Voice of Doubt.
"Nothing was ever really this simple."
"But I have proof," I say,
as I display Sarah's drawings,
a world where things happen
in primary colors.
Here in bright red marker
is a picture of me, the Mom.
I stand in a circle of hearts
smiling and holding out my arms.
Behind me the daughter
stands in a smaller circle
joined with the first to make a figure eight—
"Me," says Sarah Grace.

And here are two people
sitting at a table—
a girl in pigtails and a print dress,
a man in a striped shirt and hat,
from which a blue flower grows.
Between them on the table
are good things to eat—
pink drinks with red straws
and bright food on white plates.

Here is a wedding party—
ladies in multicolored dresses,
a man with a smile that takes up his whole face—
all crowded together under some sort of arbor.
Any moment, now, you can tell
the most wonderful thing in the world
will happen.

54

Finally, here is my favorite:
a girl with piles of fruit at her sides—
purple circles of grapes,
yellow curves of bananas,
green and pink wedges of watermelon,
dotted with black seeds.
Above her head floats a fantasy of desserts—
chocolate bars and lifesavers in all colors,
popcorn and pink ice cream with a cherry.

In Sarah's world, you see,
everyone is always surrounded by good things,
and no one ever has to be alone.

"So what?" says the Voice of Doubt.
"So," I say, "I come from a world of blank spaces,
where things happen in shades of gray.
Sarah comes from me,
and these pictures come from Sarah.
This is magic enough for me."

And yet, even though we are so different, during at least her first twelve years or so, I was never entirely sure where I left off and Sarah began. Early in my life, my mother and sister had moved all the way to the other side of the country, where the rest of my female relatives already lived as well. So this perfect little girl seemed to me a gift intended to make up for all the family members I had lost. She was a very cuddly baby and an affectionate child; domestic from the beginning, at a little over a year she was toddling around covering us up with blankets and fretting in her baby English if all her family members were not present and accounted for. She was such an easy child to be close to—so different from my wiry, independent little son.

At around the time she was born, Aaron started to have serious asthma attacks, resulting in several trips to the emergency room and many sleepless nights for us. Sarah too had a croup-like ailment at one point that made her wheeze and gasp for breath. We were all lucky, however, and both children emerged from these early episodes in good health. To me, it was simply unthinkable that anything could happen to either of them.

But, of course, anything could have and anything sometimes does. In 1992, our family moved to Norfolk, Virginia, so that Jeffrey could take a job teaching in the English department of Old Dominion University. Not long after we moved, we were invited to a dinner party at the home of Shelly Wagner on the Lafayette River in one of Norfolk's older neighborhoods. One night in 1984, Shelly, then divorced, had gone out to sit and play with her five-year-old son Andrew. It was a lovely evening—mild and clear. Shelly went inside for just a few minutes to get a drink or answer the telephone, she can't remember just what now. But when she got back, Andrew was gone. Later that night his small, sodden body was found in the Lafayette River.

Several years later, Shelly began working on a book of poems that tell—in words that are clear, evocative, and devastating—the story of Andrew's life and death. She was in the final stages of editing the book for publication and asked if I would help, which I did willingly if not gladly. For me the kicker was

that I had a daughter who was exactly the age Andrew had been
when he died.

White Roses
For Shelly in celebration of *The Andrew Poems*

When it was time to go,
you filled my arms with white roses—
so many I had to cradle them
as if I held a child.

These weren't your haughty court lady kind
but open-faced dairymaid roses,
spilling in cheerful confusion
over the low stone wall—
their scent not heavy
but fresh as morning rain.

I had come to help prepare your poems,
to deliver them soft and round and whole
into a world of sharp angles and hard edges.

Eyes blurred from too much revision—
the words as meaningless
as birds' feet tracks in sand—
we stepped onto the lawn that slopes to the river,
and the world split suddenly open into water and sky.

The river glowed serenely
with the soft light of early evening,
the roses tumbling over the wall
like happy, unruly children
on their way down the lawn to the river.
I buried my nose in their blossoms

as I sometimes do in my daughter's hair:
Now, I thought, *I know why I'm here.*

After I'd brought them home
and put them in a vase,
my five-year-old daughter asked,
"Are the roses still alive?"
I just didn't know
how to answer.

In China white is the color of death, the color worn at funerals. I have never liked white roses.

A mother and her five-year-old child are not really two separate beings but are joined at the heart. I think it was so hard for Shelly to turn that manuscript over to the publisher because it was almost all she had left of Andrew. She is one of the bravest people I know. After giving a poetry reading, Shelly would find a long line of mourners waiting to talk to her—people who had lost children, siblings, or spouses. I could not have listened and talked to these people with Shelly's clarity and compassion. I could not have talked to them at all.

Into the barren and blasted landscape that was my early life, my husband and children had brought color and light and warmth. Only they could have made a world that was possible for me to inhabit; without them, I would not have survived. Probably because of my early feelings of abandonment when my birth family split up, I have always been anxious about any form of separation. Until quite recently, within the last ten years or so, I lived in a state of near-constant fear that someone I loved would be taken away from me. For example, if my husband was an hour

58

late coming home from work, I would become convinced that he had been involved in a terrible traffic accident. I never counted on having a child return home from Scout Camp or a trip with grandparents. It is only within the last few years or so that I have come to see how odd this was—now that I am no longer plagued with fears of losing my family members.

Nevertheless, separation, like its cousin death, is a fact of even a rather ordinary life. Fortunately, by the time my son was ready to go to college, I was psychically healthy enough to withstand his departure with only the usual degree of pain— which I have, however, heard other parents compare to that caused by amputation or death. The fact is that we are all deeply connected; family members make up a body that has its own integrity. The notion that each of us is a largely independent unit is one of the great fallacies of Western culture—"monadism," my husband Jeffrey calls it. Nevertheless, it is also true that each of us is on a journey; for a time our paths may come together, but inevitably they will also diverge. If the time together is well spent, however, the loss of separation is never total. Unlike Frost, I would venture to say that something gold always stays and that the ending of one journey is always the beginning of another.

Beginnings
For my students in English 112L, Fall 2000

Do you remember when the world was new
as your first box of 64 crayons—
the promise of their waxy smell,
their perfect points,

their names like burnt sienna,
yellow ochre, jungle green, sky blue,
and carnation pink?

I did as I drove my son back to college
on a mid-October morning
along the wooded avenues of his campus,
the leaves in Crayola colors
swirling down around us,
their smell sharp in our nostrils.

Do you remember how quickly
the crayons lost their points
so you had to peel away the paper
until only blunt little nubs were left?

I did as I drove back from my son's college,
the afternoon light already foreshadowing darkness,
its slant sharp as a scythe.

And I remembered another October
when I wheeled my son's stroller through piles
of fallen leaves
burnt golden as his hair.
When I got home,
I rushed up to my daughter's bedroom
and took a cigar box of crayons
out of her top desk drawer.
I fingered their papered sides
and held piles of them in my hands
as if they were pieces of gold.

Deeply I breathed in
the promise of their waxy smell—
their colors brilliant as leaves
on a mid-October morning.

60

Old Friends

The early breakup of my family, and in particular my mother's conspicuous absence, left a vacuum that begged to be filled. This has been both a curse and a blessing. Clearly, it caused me much pain and difficulty, but it also opened doors that no doubt would have remained closed if I had had the neat, airtight little life I thought I so wanted at the time. With a mother who was useful to me largely as a negative example, I had to construct my identity more or less from scratch. And the obvious direction for me to turn for this was toward my father's seven sisters.

After World War II, most of my aunts returned to California and eventually settled in or near Los Angeles. It's just as well that they grew up in this country because I can't imagine seven such strong-minded women having an easy time of it in the repressive atmosphere of early twentieth-century Japan. Nevertheless, they retained some of the clannishness of their cultural heritage, and to this day they are constantly visiting, helping, and fussing over each other—which is probably how five out of seven have stayed alive for so long (the oldest is now ninety-six). One of those no longer living is Ina Ito, who suffered a miscarriage in a stable on the way to Amache, Colorado, where she was being "detained" during the Second World War—and who thereafter was never able to have children of her own. Perhaps this also helps explain why she was also the only one of the sisters who seemed chronically anxious and unhappy to me; the others are all notably upbeat most of the time.

When I was a small child, my father would sometimes fly with me across the country to see my Japanese family. He was a favorite brother and son, and I quickly became a favorite niece and granddaughter. Suddenly I, virtually motherless at home, found myself fussed over by eight women—my grandmother and her seven daughters. A misfit in Chapel Hill, I slipped effortlessly into my place in the family during the reunions held at my Auntie Gogo's beautiful old house in Los Angeles. I loved my uncles too—especially my Uncle Foof (George Fujii that is; everyone had a nickname), who, in his terrible English, delighted in trying to persuade me to eat sashimi. But the men who married my aunts were no match for the Sugioka sisters, by whom they had all clearly been cowed into meekest submission long ago. According to my father, my aunts paid me the ultimate compliment during a family gathering several years ago when, in commenting on something I'd said or done, one of them remarked, "Stephanie is a real Sugioka." I can picture them perfectly—seven tiny women (none is over five feet) nodding in agreement at this statement of indisputable fact, huddling over sink or cutting board as they worked together to prepare one of the feasts that appear as if by magic every time the family comes together.

Our visits were rare. Time was short and plane fares expensive. And I have never been able to afford to see them as often as I would like. Still, they were there, and the mere fact of their presence in the world helped me more than they could have known.

Los Angeles

There they were
all during my lonely childhood
in a small southern East Coast town—

62

shimmering softly
on some far horizon
like a host of lost angels.
Ah, but on our trips west
they'd gather, a bright band, around us,
and I knew I was really
a Japanese princess
come home to my true throne
in the high castle of their regard.

They were not ethereal creatures, though,
but solid and sure as rivers and mountains:

      Auntie Mamie, a buyer for a big department store,
      intuitively knew of your need
      for four pairs of pajamas.
      She could outfit you completely
      with accessories to match
      in thirty minutes flat.

      Auntie Ina hovered and fussed,
      patted and nagged
      (you could almost hear the nervous whirr
      of her wings),
      her sushi much more beautiful
      than most works of modern art.

      Auntie Dora slips from room to room
      serving five-course meals from her tiny kitchen.
      She is small and lovely
      as a Japanese doll,
      her life as serene as a tea ceremony.

      Auntie Gogo, true to her name,
      always just back from an African safari,
      a tour of Japan,

an Alaskan expedition.
She taught English
and brooked no nonsense.

Auntie Arlie glows softly
and roundly like a Buddha,
devoted to her Down syndrome son,
her one great calling to be beloved by all.
Auntie Mary, the churchmouse,
always the last to be noticed,
still, though legally blind,
sends my children presents
she makes by hand for Christmas.

Auntie Lillie inclines her head
and flowers arrange themselves,
bread dough rises to attention.
The eldest, she is as poised
as a lotus on a long cool stem.
And down her spine there runs
a fine thread of Samurai steel.

And so this constellation of sisters
shone bright in the wide night skies
of my childhood.
Cast adrift far east of California,
I used them to find my way

as a sailor uses the stars:
celestial navigation.

My aunts are growing older.
One by one they fade
like stars as morning approaches.
But I know that on some farther shore

they'll be waiting
to show me how to come home.

Once I came quite close to living on the West Coast near my aunts. Shortly after my parents' divorce in 1965, my father was offered a good job as a professor of anesthesiology at the University of Washington in Seattle. I had been looking forward to the move; it seemed like a chance to be near my relatives and to start over after my parents' doomed marriage had ended. Having grown up in a small town in the Southeast, I was also curious about what life would be like in a city in the Pacific Northwest. My mother, however, objected and threatened to get a court order barring my father from taking my brother and me out of state. She got her way, and we stayed in Chapel Hill. Yet less than a year later, she herself moved with my little sister to Berkeley, California, to pursue a degree in design at the university there. So having deprived me and my brother of the chance to live near our aunts, she then deprived us of her own company and our sister's as well. Had she not prevented my father from moving us to Seattle, we could have all lived on the same coast if not in the same state. Her behavior seemed to me spitefully perverse and deeply irrational, and I wanted to have nothing to do with it.

Nevertheless, her absence left spaces in my life into which others could enter. For seven years during my late teens and early twenties, I dated a man whose mother opened her arms and her heart to me without reserve. Her name was Dorothy Westafer—she was a dancer, an artist, and a high school drama teacher. She

65

died when I was in my late twenties, and it has taken me a lifetime to realize how rare was her combination of warmth, wisdom, and artistic accomplishment and how very lucky I was that she came into my life at the moment I most needed a mother. When I was an undergraduate at Goucher College, I met Eleanor Wilner, English professor and poet, who inspired me, mentored me, and helped me to publish my first feeble little poems; she remains my loyal friend to this day. When my son was born, I would have been terribly isolated and depressed if it had not been for the working-class couple, Arnold and Verona Duchrow, who rented us the apartment above their house in Plymouth, Wisconsin; having few material advantages themselves, they were incredibly generous to us and became devoted substitute grandparents to our son. Friends in Chapel Hill, North Carolina—Ken and Pattie McIntyre—who were renting us the house next to theirs when my daughter was born, filled a similar role later on. Pattie died only recently, leaving behind countless mourners who remember her gracious hospitality and her expression of perpetual amazed delight at all the books and people and places she encountered. A reference librarian at the graduate library of UNC, Chapel Hill, she was also a true southern lady; I never knew her to utter a thoughtless word or to perform a petty act. So this is my company of saints, and no doubt, in some strange way, I have my mother to thank for the blessing of their presence in my life.

The wonderful thing about friendship, of course, is its nonobligatory nature. We often do not require our friends to do anything in particular but just to be there for us—to keep us easy company on life's frequently hard and wearisome journey. We may not be able to choose our family members, but we can, to some degree, choose our friends. And yet sometimes the most meaningful relationships turn out to be not those we choose but those that just happen to us. When I moved with my family to Chesapeake, Virginia in 1992, we left behind a Congregational church where we had had a number of friends and where we had been quite happy. We visited ten churches in our new community but found none that felt right. Finally, we attended a little Disciples of Christ church only a few miles from where we lived; it was a real country church, many of its members were related and had attended it most of their lives. Interestingly, the Disciples church had been that of my father's family—probably one of the few that welcomed Japanese immigrants in those days. It is a church that seems to accommodate individualists—those who do not easily follow rules that are too numerous or rigid—and this little church was no exception. It had more than its share of genuine characters. But the spirit was right, and it was perfectly exemplified by the young man for whom this poem was written.

In Memory of Ti

So many things he didn't have:
a car in the garage,
letters after his name,
bills, doubts, ambitions,
a job, a wife, a child—
all the trappings thought necessary
to make you somebody.

A few things he had
and loved
with all his simple heart:
his videotapes of old movies,
his Mickey Mouse tie and suspenders,
his season tickets to operas,
his father, his sisters,
his church, his God.

His body, wrong from birth,
ordained a life of pain:
endless drugs and needles,
procedures and operations.
His pale cheeks never grew hair.
His large head wobbled like a flower
too heavy for its stem,
eyes the clear high blue
of an early summer sky.

Without the usual clutter,
his life held plenty of space
for us.
He was always ready to listen,
to crack a joke about his condition,
to describe the T-shirt his sister
had given him for Christmas,
to assure us of the many blessings
of God.

Near the end
when he lay in his hospital bed,
his sister tried to pull a sheet over his legs
all mottled from needles and blocked circulation.
"Don't cover my rainbow legs," he said.

Already he knew he belonged
to the sky.

We bookish types form some of our closest relationships
with people whose faces we've never seen, whose voices we've
never heard; and sometimes we think we know them better than
those with whom we sit down at the dinner table. My husband
Jeffrey has virtually made a career of salvaging from the past
obscure writers who would otherwise have been lost altogether.
Once we made a trip to Massachusetts, for example, to follow the
trail of the Revolutionary era writer Mercy Otis Warren. We
visited her house, her grave, and her town. For a while, it really
did seem that we could feel her presence at our dinner table—and
a stern presence it was too.

Oddly—and even though there are many women writers
I admire—my literary parents are almost all men—Keats, Yeats,
Whitman, and Eliot. I sometimes wonder if this is because I was
raised by a man. Or perhaps it is because men are easier to pin
down—or at least give us the illusion they are. This is one of the
subjects of the poem that follows. I am actually not that fond of
Van Gogh but much prefer the American Impressionists;
however, this poem demanded to be written, and I complied as
best I could.

Van Gogh in a Form of Limitation: Self-Portrait, 1887

The air, you see, had begun
to thicken like drying paint around him.
It wrinkles around his head like oil
flecked with blood the red of his beard.

69

From the faraway look in his eyes,
you can tell he's given up
trying to claw his way out.

Jeanne Calment, the world's oldest person
at a hundred and twenty years and some,
remembers selling him colored pencils
at her father's shop in Arles.
"He was ugly, ill-tempered, and reeked of wine,"
she said. He had a gift for art, Mme Calment for life:
"A good God has forgotten me," she says.
But clearly God did not forget Van Gogh.

For here he is in the calendar on my wall,
looking out across the no-man's land of years.
Shortly before his death, in a shop in Arles,
he failed to notice how the slanting light
fell on the glossy braid of the little girl
who held out the colored pencils he'd come to buy,
the smell of fresh air and soap
rising from the sprigged muslin of her dress.

The life of Jeanne Calment flows away
like a little river in sunlight,
soon to disappear from sight.

But good old Van Gogh is still with us—
"Mon semblable,—mon frère!"

After This, Our Exile

With the notable exception of a year spent in Beijing, China (1984-
85), I spent the years of 1979 to 1986 in Wisconsin. As I've said, I
regarded my situation during that time as one of exile. During my

70

years growing up in Chapel Hill, digging in its red clay and playing in its woods and streams, the landscape became a part of me. After almost seven years in Wisconsin, I was sick to death of the flat landscape and the brutal winters. I wanted to go home. It was easy to persuade my husband, who was by this time weary of his grueling dead-end job at a small college, where he kept accumulating additional responsibilities without any accompanying benefits. So with no job prospects and virtually no money, we packed up our small household, strapped our four-year-old son into his carseat in our battered brown Toyota station wagon, and came back to Chapel Hill—the place where I had been raised and we had married. As sometimes happens when one takes what looks like a very stupid risk, things worked out beautifully. Out of the blue, Jeffrey was offered a one-year visiting professorship at the University of North Carolina, old friends from Jeffrey's grad school days let us stay at their house while they were traveling during the summer, and eventually we found a house in a lovely wooded neighborhood to rent (our landlord and landlady were old friends and colleagues of my parents).

It is often said that you can't go home again, but in some very real way, I did. Our six years in Chapel Hill were not always comfortable ones, but they were profoundly healing. I had several run-ins with my father and stepmother, who still lived there, but in the process I resolved some important issues—most notably my pain and resentment at what I perceived as their abandonment of me and my brother when they started their new family. Jeffrey and I went into counseling together and laid some of our old ghosts to rest as well. Finally, our daughter Sarah Grace was born, and this event alone seemed to redeem all my losses at once—my neglectful mother, my missing sister, my marital difficulties. This may seem hard to believe, but it is certainly not the first time the birth of a child has worked such miracles.

The only problem was that we couldn't stay. It must be in the nature of such Edens (ironically, this was the name of the two pastors at our church in Chapel Hill) that eventually one has to set back off down that long hot road into the desert or the wilderness or, God forbid, the suburbs (and this is exactly what happened to us). However, I left with a much greater trust in the world and much surer sense of myself than I had come with, and this is the subject of my next poem.

Leaving Chapel Hill

I go out from this green womb
where the sun sifts down
through layers of leaves—
maple, dogwood, and oak.
These trees have rocked me and reared me.
In winter you can see they are rooted
in the sky, their branches reaching higher
than the noblest human thought.
In the beginning, there was no feta cheese,
no smoked salmon, no pâté de foie gras;
there were no spas, breast implants, frequent flyer miles.
In the beginning there were no garage sales,
no blue-light specials, no three-for-a-dollar deals,
no Fun Fruits, no skateboards, no Teenage Mutant Ninja anything.

72

In the beginning
a barefoot girl in a thin nightgown
stepped onto the soft wet lawn.
The myriad leaves of dogwood, camellia,
redbud and azalea
called my name in their many tongues.
Misty wisteria blurred the days into nights,
and honeysuckle wove spells
that turned fat toads
on plush grass
to princes on velvet pillows.

In the beginning was Morgan Creek,
long and brown as its name.
I crouched for hours on its bank,
a little maple and a mossy rock
nearby for company,
my playthings frogs and tadpoles,
crayfish and salamanders.

I took these sacred creatures back to the house
where I tried to recreate for them
the perfect life of the woods.
But they died in the still, dead water
of the aquarium, among the rotting leaves.
They must have needed the holy touch of the stream
to keep them alive.

My father still lives in a house
overlooking Morgan Creek.
I bring my children back to visit.
The walls resound with my son's hard rock,
and my daughter's laughter threads the rooms
like a little silver stream.

Sitting on a rock by the creek,
I gaze upstream.
I imagine that if I look hard enough
I can recapture the moment
before my exile.

And as I watch the water
playing over the rocks,
I become the barefoot girl
stepping onto the wet grass.
I hold out my arms
and the river rushes toward me,
like a mother, like a child.

Leaving Chapel Hill again was hard. I imagined I could hear the ripping sound of tearing roots as we packed up our household to leave. I had injured my back while lifting my daughter from rock to rock in the middle of the South Toe River (the one bordering my parents' mountain property), and the moving exacerbated the injury. By the time we moved into our new house in Chesapeake, Virginia, the pain was excruciating.

My husband had accepted a position as assistant professor of English at Old Dominion University in Norfolk, but we couldn't actually afford to buy a house in the city, and I was determined we were going to live in a house we owned ourselves. The one we bought in Chesapeake, essentially the suburbs of Norfolk, would be the first one of our married lives. It was also the first house that I could really call my own since my parents' divorce almost thirty years earlier.

Fortunately, the house we bought was in relatively good condition because neither my husband nor I am particularly handy. It was quite ordinary—a two-story with a living room, dining room, and kitchen downstairs and four smallish bedrooms upstairs. I think we were attracted more by the yard than by the house itself, and once I finally had a bit of earth to myself, I discovered that, like my father, I was a gardener at heart.

The Summer Kingdom

So it all comes down to this:
  A two-story brick house
  with garage and large deck
  on a half-acre lot in the suburbs.

I was raised in a forest Eden,
my earliest memories red camellias
floating in crystal bowls,
dogwood white in a sea
of redbud and new green.

Even now in my native town
my father lives in a house of wood
designed to fade to the silver
of the surrounding trees,
built on a hill overlooking a stream

where masses of pink rhododendron
blossom every April.

Still, I'm not surprised to find myself here,
having long accepted exile
as my natural condition.

But I can't help chafing
at the state of my neighbors' yards:
the one bare except for a lawn,
by now mostly weeds,
that my neighbor occasionally mows
to resemble the head of an ugly kid
with a buzz cut;
the other bare even of lawn,
since, for want of something better to do
the two dogs there have completely dug it up—
a mudhole in rain,
a cracked desert in drier weather.
By comparison our place doesn't look so bad—
the house flanked by two tall magnolias,
large willow oaks in front and back,
a cedar, a dogwood, some pines.

When we first moved here in the fall
we planted bulbs and a few more trees—
a maple, an apple, a weeping cherry.
It took an act of faith to put them—
then no more than sticks—into the ground.
But, lo, in spring their leaves popped out
and the flower bulbs bloomed in waves of color—
daffodils, hyacinths, irises, and lilies.

Now in summer
the gracious magnolia
lifts up huge blossoms
as cool and lemony
as a mother's hand
on a sweaty little forehead.
The mourning doves coo
long blue corridors
through the white-hot days,

and cicadas build high
round towers of sound
to create a summer kingdom.

Now at forty-two,
the first time in my vagabond life,
I dare to plant something in the ground,
and count on being around
to see it come up in the spring.

It all comes down to this:
earth's body,
broken for us
into half-acre lots
in the suburbs—
these our only
gardens

Although I now owned my own home, still the suburbs felt like a place of exile—all our planting like an effort to create a garden in a desert. I am sure some suburbs are truly nice places to live, but our suburb felt like a wasteland. The largest problem was, I think, that everyone moved too often. After eight years, we were the longest-term residents on our block. Why invest yourself in your house and yard or in your neighbors if you're going to be moving next year? People did not feel themselves to be rooted in the earth or deeply connected to their neighbors. Even in the nicer sections, where the yards were beautifully landscaped and tended and where residents often stayed longer, a sense of desolation prevailed even on a lovely spring afternoon. The beautiful yards were empty and silent. Where were the residents? Busy, I suppose, with jobs or soccer practice, and even if they were home, there was the lure of computer games and elaborate entertainment systems. In such an environment, my family members were complete misfits. During all that time, I made only one real friend there, and my children's luck was not much better. So we focused our attentions on each other and on Norfolk and Old Dominion University, where I was now teaching part time, and continued to work on our garden.

Faith

In last summer's drought
the little fir
that grew near our front steps
died.
And so this spring
in the space it left,
I decided to plant coreopsis from seed.
I was drawn to the picture

of the intricate golden flowers on the packet—
perennials that would "bloom the first year."

After I'd dug up the soil
to make the bed,
I saw I'd made a raw black wound
in the earth.
So this is why no one else plants from seed—
why my neighbors fill their new beds
with ready grown plants so quickly.

And now I can only wait.
Anxious for some sign of life
I check the round bed
that looks like a freshly dug grave
for a family pet.
When a few sprouts finally emerge,
they are hopelessly nondescript.
I can't even pull up the weeds—
I don't know which they are.
All I can do is go on
and water the weeds with the flowers.

Not here the explosion of golden blooms
that should have crowned my labors,
the stunning image that should have completed
this poem.

Only this raw black earth,
these tiny green leaves,
this long dark ache in the heart.

Fact is, I brought to the business of gardening and home ownership a whole set of clichés that quickly foundered on the rocks of reality. In my misguided drive to make my yard perfect, I slaved for subtle beauty and absolute symmetry. Naturally, my best efforts were often foiled by drought, flood, and various uncooperative creatures like earwigs, aphids, slugs, moles, and voles. Voles, for example, managed to kill a formerly thriving nandina and a lush wisteria by eating out the roots, and slugs were ruthless in their pursuit of my chrysanthemums. Interestingly, the coreopsis that is the subject of the previous poem did eventually explode into golden blooms and continued to do so for the next couple of years or so. Thus we see that truth can be not just stranger but occasionally even more beautiful than fiction.

Not long before we moved from our house in the suburbs, the symmetry of our yard was in fact completely destroyed by an old man who lost control of his car, which ran into our yard, almost leveling a beautiful set of bushes that included a holly and a crepe myrtle. Interestingly, had the bushes not halted the car, it would have crashed into the living room of the house next door, where two small children lived. I was very unhappy to lose the beautiful bushes but was forced to   I was less sure about the joys of home ownership than I was about my feelings for the yard. In my previous experience, houses had mostly been the setting of much misery, most notably that caused by the domestic conflict in my early childhood. Specifically, I remember the dark, narrow stairs, down which my mother claimed my father had pushed her and the gash in the linoleum floor that had resulted from one of my mother's dish-throwing tantrums. The Chapel Hill house had had many dark corners—a dank basement, for example, that included a room called the "no-no room," where many rusty, dirty, and generally unidentifiable objects lived. We children were solemnly warned of the terrible dangers of that basement room, and we believed every word we heard.

In my dreams, bad things always happened in houses. Generally, if I was able to escape the dangers of the house, I was home free. This next poem reflects this ambivalence.

80

They Got It Wrong in Genesis
For Aaron

What really happened is this:
In the beginning, Adam and Eve had fur
as soft and thick as a rabbit's.
But then they disobeyed and ate the apple,
using their new toy—
the knowledge of good and evil—
to classify and divide their world without end,
and placing, in the larger scheme of things
humans at the top, animals near the bottom.

Catching them at their game,
God stripped them of their fur,
leaving them pink and naked as newborn rats.
"So you think you're that much better
than my furred and feathered creatures?" God said.
"Then go and dwell in a separate place."
And ever since then, we've lived in the exile
of houses.

The problem with houses is
most of them are too dark inside,
and except for us, some germs and dustmites
(and maybe a stray ant or cockroach),
everything in them is dead.
No wonder, then, that we're such a morbid race.

And now when we go outdoors,
nature exacts its revenge
for the arrogance of our forbears:
cold chills or sun burns,
bees sting, mosquitoes bite,
and we retreat indoors where it's safe and deadly.

But on a day like this one in early fall,
when the rabbits hop to the front of their hutch to be petted
and sunlight touches your hair with grace;
when you can bury your face in a cushion of yellow
chrysanthemum blossoms,
each one pressing against your skin like a kiss —

On a day like this,
God suffers us
not to be separated
but welcomes us back —
if just for this moment —
into the land of the living.

So life in a house in the suburbs was to me a kind of exile within an exile. In my naiveté, however, I thought that I could make everything better if I would only just work a little harder. So I painted walls, dug out weeds, and had the neighbors over for backyard cookouts even when my invitations weren't returned. During the last few years there, however, I think I was beginning to understand the futility of my efforts. This message was reinforced for me when I recently returned to the neighborhood and drove by our old house to see what changes had or hadn't been made. I barely recognized the yard. The house was the same, but subsequent owners had removed from the yard almost every single tree or shrub that had made the place distinctive—the dogwood, the redbud, the Japanese maple, and the amazing crabapple tree that had filled the front yard with blossoms in the spring—all gone. Only the magnolias, which had probably been too large and costly to remove, had been allowed to stay. And yet

I remember so clearly how, at certain times of year, our yard truly
looked like a garden in the desert.

Late Afternoon in Early Spring
Is it possible to live without feasting on death?
—Walker Percy, *Love in the Ruins*

It's one of those days when the air's so light and warm
your body feels like dandelion fluff,
a day when there's no point in doing a thing—
for what could match the forsythia's grace,
the pink camellia's perfection, the generosity
of white crab apple blossoms?
And so I'm content to lie in my hammock
breathing in the smell of new-mown grass.

My Japanese neighbor hangs her wash on the line.
Lovely and slim, black hair to her waist,
she slips between the clothes and sheets
like a sliver of moon through clouds.
She spends her time studying English,
as she waits for her navy husband's return.
But her English never seems to improve,
and she misses her family in Japan.

The two little Indian girls from next door
speaking in soft English accents
wander through the overgrown grass of their yard
in long red and blue print dresses.
(Their mother, plump and smelling of cooking,
stays inside and tries to hide
from America, but what she sees on her telly
only confirms that dangers lurk
around every corner, behind every bush.)

Our other next-door neighbor works for the power company.
Here he is, large and white, on his red riding mower
his body overflowing the small seat.
When he's not mowing his lawn,
he spends his time trying to revive
the VCR, weedeater, toaster oven—
one dead machine or another—
his wife at a mall or garage sale
shopping for the one last item
that will make their lives complete.

Their two small children, a boy and girl,
are often left to themselves.
When they're not watching TV
they trail around their backyard
clutching Barbies and Power Rangers,
their pale faces wet with mucus and tears,
wailing like little lost spirits.

I used to try to get all my neighbors together
for potluck suppers or cookouts,
but someone was always busy—
my Japanese neighbor waiting for a phone call,
my Indian ones for a relative's visit,
my American ones for the plumber.

So I turned to my yard instead,
planting every inch with bushes and flowers.
But when I dug too deep, I uncovered
a network of thick white roots,
their surfaces stained with red,
their source a mystery.
It's getting late, but I hate to go in—
such afternoons are so rare.
Against the chainlink fence

the pyracantha stretches
thorny, twisted branches,
and the columbine close by
drips endless red and white blossoms.
The last rays of sunlight linger—
touching the crab apple's trunk,
the chainlink fence, the camellia petals,
the lawnmower seat, the blades of new grass—
like the fingers
of a dying
savior.

And yet, our eight years in the suburbs were not a total loss after all. Finding little to attract us to our immediate surroundings, the members of our family drew closer to one another. My son and daughter had been ten and five when we'd moved to Chesapeake. Up to that time they'd had little to do with each other. My son when he was nine, for example, could not see what relevance a four-year-old upstart female could possibly have to his existence. But by the time we left Chesapeake eight years later, Aaron and Sarah had become good friends. After dinner, the four of us, would sit around the table talking and laughing uproariously about next to nothing, Jeff and I being only slightly less silly than the children. Our last year in Chesapeake was also Aaron's last year at home. The summer of our move to Norfolk, he went on to attend college at William and Mary in Williamsburg. So our last year in Chesapeake was also in some ways our last year together as a family.

After Eight Years of Suburban Living

The cookie jar wasn't always full
or the neighbors particularly friendly.
My daughter's room was usually a mess
and sometimes my son's heavy metal
sounded as if it might saw the house in two.

But late one summer afternoon
as I stood at the second-story window
the green of grass and willow and pine
deepening to dusk,
a dozen fireflies lit up at once—

as if someone had tossed a handful of stars
onto the darkening lawn.

Of Wind and Wood

In the spring of 1982 when I was eight months pregnant with my son Aaron, I had to take a set of grueling exams for my Master's degree in Chinese literature at the University of Wisconsin. I was by this time living about a hundred miles away, and I had to commute back to Madison to take the exams. As women usually are in their ninth month of pregnancy, I was tired almost all the time. The exams lasted between three and four hours and included an additional essay that I had not prepared for. By the time I wrote my last word, I was so exhausted I could hardly speak. When I later talked to other students in my program who had also taken the exams, I discovered that they had not had to write the last essay. Apparently it had been added to my exam

86

especially for my benefit. The professors who devised the exam were, of course, all men.

Sexism in our society is so obvious that it seems almost unnecessary to talk about it. For those of us born in the fifties, it was in the air we breathed and the water we drank. Granted that it has become less prevalent and less obvious during the last few years, but it is still alive and well in subtle as well as not-so-subtle forms. I would be very surprised to learn from a female peer that she has not at some time been bullied by a male boss or held to a higher standard than male students by a male professor. What complicates the situation for me is that I was largely raised by a male parent.

As far as I can tell, men often dominate and bully women because they feel threatened by them. Since men are in many ways so obviously the more privileged sex, I find this hard to understand but can only speculate that at some primitive level, many men must be jealous of women's power to procreate, to give birth to a living child. When I realized that my professors must have constructed an exam for me that was longer and more difficult than the ones my classmates took, I couldn't help thinking that this jealousy was the motive.

As a single father at a time when there so few others like him, my father did his best, and I never doubted that he loved me. But at times, his treatment of me seemed unnecessarily harsh. At these times, I felt as if I had bumped into something in an otherwise warm and nurturing sea that was old and cold, dark and hard. Thus this poem:

Janus's Daughter
For Patti Holt

In the beginning,
our father
stood looking out his doorway,
but disgusted by the chaos of creation,
he turned to stare forever
into the darkness of his house.

He wanted to keep me in.
But like a sliver of moon
I slipped past him.
And the light came laughing
after me
like a crowd of noisy children.

Not only was I raised by a man, but my literary fathers
were males as well. Of course, there are many women poets and
writers whose works I love and admire: Lady Murasaki, Jane
Austen, Mary Oliver, and Eleanor Wilner, to name a few. But the
writers I studied early on were those who most influenced my
writing and, I think, continue to do so, and they were the likes of
T. S. Eliot, John Keats, W. B. Yeats, and Walt Whitman. Of course
this gave me much to choose from: Eliot's spirituality, Keats's
passion, Yeats's ingenuity, and Whitman's expansiveness. But, as
this next poem makes, clear, I have not always been comfortable
in the knowledge that these men were my literary forbears:

Return

Old TSE, your words
rattle around in my head
like dry seeds in a gourd.
I am a child at the gate.
Will the veiled sister pray for me?
(Behind me she walks in white and blue
her finger pressed to her lips.
We must be still to hear
the dry whisper of your will.)

I wait outside your garden
with an overwhelming question:
Will these seeds live?
Will the water from your fountain
quench my thirst?
Will the branches of your trees
hold my weight?
Will their apples satisfy my hunger?
When you hear my laughter, will you turn
even if you do not hope
and hold your arms up
so that I can climb down?

My mother was not given to gestures of affection. Most of
the time she hardly seemed to notice me, but when she did, I never
knew whether she was going to kiss me or smack me. The first
time a woman ever held my head to her breast and comforted me,
it was my own daughter at the age of about thirteen. The feeling
of those soft arms around me and that warm heart beating so close

my face was a revelation. Before my daughter was born, my father very much hoped I would have a girl. So did I.

      Early Spring
      For Sarah Grace

Bent with the weight of winter
the crab-apple tree spreads over our front yard,
branches impossibly twisted
as if in long and convoluted thought.

But on this first warm morning
fog catches on stiff gray limbs
growing clusters of tiny leaves.

Somewhere an old man
puts down his newspaper,
looks out the window,
and thinks for a moment
of his granddaughter.

How Can I Keep from Singing?

When I was little, my father taught me, on long car trips, almost all the songs he knew; they included "Red Sails on the Sunset," "Beautiful Ohio," "Just a Song at Twilight," and "Tell Me Why," among many others. I would lie on the living room rug listening to stereo recordings of *Carousel*, *South Pacific*, and *Oklahoma*, faithfully memorizing the words to every song. This has proved a great embarrassment to my family, because I have a song for almost any occasion and am apt to burst into song at the least

90

provocation. I have a good sense of pitch and the kind of soprano voice—pure but not very loud—that is perfect for church choirs, in many of which I've sung. I have sung solos on occasion, but my voice is not operatic enough to be very impressive. My father's favorite music is, of course, opera.

But, anyway, I love to sing and continue to do so whether there is anyone to hear me or not. No matter what I am doing or where I am, there is usually a song playing somewhere in the back of my head; sometimes it is the hymn by Robert Lowry from which the title of this chapter is taken, three stanzas and the refrain of which go as follows:

My life flows on in endless song
Above earth's lamentation
I hear the clear though far-off hymn
That hails a new creation.
No storm can shake my inmost calm
As to that rock I'm clinging.
Since love is lord of heaven and earth,
How can I keep from singing? (Refrain)

Above the tumult and the strife
I hear that music ringing.
It finds an echo in my soul.
How can I keep from singing?

The peace of Christ makes fresh my heart,
A fountain ever springing.
All things are mine if I am his.
How can I keep from singing?

It has a lovely folklike tune, and I wish I could sing it for you. I hope someone will sing it at my funeral.

So the song is the subtext of all I do and am. It helps me to reconcile my ideal world with the real one. When I was much younger, these two were very different things that I could not make fit together no matter how hard I tried:

The Real Thing

I was miserable in those days
but rather beautiful—
straight dark hair to my waist
big brown eyes with a slight exotic tilt
slim as a wood nymph
all sunlight and shadow.

Then, though,
the whole world seemed negotiable—
more or less.
An actress off and on
I played the Young Lady
in Strindberg's *Ghost Sonata*,
slowly dying
in a pool
of lavender light.
I thought the world
a stage,
my life a perpetual dress rehearsal
for the real performance to come.
The world as it was
did not meet my specifications,
but I assumed that elsewhere
on some other plane

92

life was proceeding just as it should:
I had a lovely cookie-baking mother,
a father who took me on special trips to D.C.
and to the sweetheart banquet.
No wonder that as I walked
down my dormitory hall,
my footsteps sounded so hollow,
so unreal.

Was it when I first went into labor—
a huge fist shaking my body
as if it were a ragdoll,
bolts of lightening charging
up and down my spine—
that I understood
this was no dress rehearsal?

When they laid my son Aaron in my arms—
his mouth a small black hole
searching for my breast,
his dark, enormous eyes
devouring my face—

I must have understood
there was no other,
ideal form of Aaron.

Yes, it must have been at this moment
I knew I was playing for keeps.

So the two worlds collided, or rather, I realized that there had
never been two but only one—this one. I have spent the last
twenty-three years since Aaron's birth trying to learn that there
really is no moment but the present moment, no place but this
place, no people but these people. With a hyperactive mind that
wants to leap back into the past, plunge forward into the future,

or go spinning off into the stratosphere, I have found this a very hard lesson to learn; but having my daughter seems to have helped.

Now

The people pass—their voices rise and fall.
Sarah wakes not feeling well today.
The world goes by in shadows on her wall.

She covers her head with her afghan and curls up small.
Light shines through in red and blue and gold.
The people pass—their voices rise and fall.

The door slams shut—she hears her father call.
Sun bright, wind high—tree branches toss and sway.
The world goes by in shadows on her wall.

The telephone rings shrilly down the hall.
She lies beneath her afghan warm and still.
The people pass—their voices rise and fall.

Like sun and water, Sarah's thoughts are all
she needs to make bright flowers bloom and twine.
The world goes by in shadows on her wall.

With her stillness, softly she enthralls
the moment like a fawn in sunlit glade.
The people pass—their voices rise and fall.
The world goes by in shadows on her wall.

My father, my model in all things when I was younger, was an extrovert par excellence. He was an anesthesiologist—really, as I later learned, a sort of expert technician. To him the physical world was the only world, and he has traveled to every corner of
94

the globe—Alaska, Africa, Japan, and Europe—to partake of its pleasures and witness its wonders. He does not read, write, or think very deeply. To him, the inner world is nonexistent. My daughter, on the other hand, is a creature of interiors. She has a large dollhouse that her father made her, decorated in the Victorian style with a piano that plays a tune if wound up, a perfect mahogany dining room table, and all the trappings— curtains, dishes, and tiny toys for the perfect little Victorian doll children. She has wanted to be an interior designer since she was ten. I am reminded of the Bronte sisters, who wrote whole books on pages the size of postage stamps.

For me, it is music, song, that reveals the inner world and makes the "real" world bearable.

Jazz Trio

In the cold hard air of November
the concert hall fills with a warm sea of sound.
The bass player plumbs the depths of the water,
the swish of the drums like sunlight brushing waves,
the piano arpeggios a school of bright fish
darting into the coral.

The broad-shouldered bass player
pulls his bow over the strings—
the muscles of the music.
The sticks of the long-limbed drummer
seem to come from his bones.
The bird of a man perched at the piano
trills, and the blood

moves through the body
till it sways in its chains like the sea.

No Handel or Bach,
picky about beginnings, middles, and ends,
this music flows on like an everlasting stream,
like a carpet of stars unrolling
through the darkness.
Mercer, Brown, Porter, Corea—
It could go on forever.

This is music to dive in,
a big warm mama, who wraps you in her arms
and rocks you, chanting your name
over and over like the sea.

I came to this concert
from a cold, dry world,
my heart as shriveled
as a Japanese mushroom.
But now
it springs from its shell
like the paper flowers
we used to drop into water—
bursting into blossom.

In one of my earlier poems, "Allegro con Spirito," I talk
about the taste of a song. In that poem, song becomes a sort of
communion wafer. The song truly is the word made flesh. The
following poem is dedicated to Eleanor Wilner, who taught me
almost all I know about poetry and who loved to hear me sing:

Blueberries
For Eleanor

We had to fight the birds for them,
surrounding the bushes with nets
so that we could only pick them
one at a time
reaching thumb and forefinger
through the mesh
like the beak of a bird.

The berries felt
round and soft and firm
as nipples,
worth the blood
the mosquitoes sucked
from our arms and legs
as we picked.
And in spite of the four
tablespoons of cornstarch,
when I cut the pie
I'd made with the berries,
the purple filling rose
and stained the white flesh of the crust,
flowing onto the dessert plate
smelling of earth and sunlight
tasting so sharp and sweet
it sliced my tongue into song.

Like Whitman, I sing a song of myself, but unlike his, my
song is softer, harder to hear, like the murmur of a hidden stream.
I envy him his expansiveness, his ability to encompass nations,
worlds, the universe. He was, of course, a great lover of music,
but not of the little song—rather, of the loud, the magnificent, the

operatic. And, of course, like so many other writers, I had to write a poem to honor him:

Father of Waters
For Walt

I've been down to Bennett's Creek
to look for you.
I crouched among the laurel
and heard you speak
in the rattle of the last brown beech leaves.
I saw the river come loafing
around the bend,
the sun strike every blade of marsh grass
into fire.

Though you loafed and lounged, you were
intense as an egret's beak,
finely strung as a Stradivarius.
And the fingers of all the waters
plucked your strings,
the mouths of all the rivers
murmured your name—
Elizabeth, Lafayette, Nansemond, James.
Whether queen or commoner,
hero or slave,
you answered.
You opened your arms
and the long silver rivers flowed through you,
the wind, crazy with spring,
filled your lungs with song.

I went down into the streets
among the people you love

and listened for your voice.
I heard that the Dow was down ten points,
that I could buy one, get one free,
that sixteen Palestinians were shot by Israeli troops
(or was it the other way around?)
and someone kept shouting about Jesus.
But I never heard your voice.
So I've come back to the marshes,
where the streams are your shining arms,
reaching out to hold me,
the grass your springy hair,
breathing its heady, rank perfume,
the wind your endless voice
calling, so softly,
come home.

Shall We Gather at the River?

Asked about his or her family or community, probably any red-blooded American would be quick to tell you how important they are. But look around you. How close are, say, most teenagers really to their families? How much are most people really an integral part of their communities? I've lived in only two other countries for any length of time—Germany and communist China, to be exact—but from my limited experience, I would say that this is the loneliest country in the world—and getting lonelier all the time. Witness the opportunities for online banking and self-checkout stations at Walmart. I don't think there is anything more important to most people's sense of well-being than the touch of another's hand, the sound of a human voice. But these are increasingly hard to come by in our profit-driven, electronically mediated society. Is loneliness truly the necessary price of independence, of individualism? If so, it seems too steep a price to pay.

And what about those rare occasions when we do come together? I was taught to be a good Japanese-American hostess. This meant, of course, that everything had to be picture perfect—the house, the food, the conversation—and if anything was "imperfect," the occasion was, by my lights, a complete failure. My poor husband used to feel terrorized by the preparations for a dinner party, and I can hardly blame him:

Dinner for Six
or
A Tragedy of Comic Proportions
For Janet Peery

It was one of those nights—
The oysters wouldn't open,
the sauce wouldn't thicken,
and the phone rang just
as I was serving dinner.

The magician who could salvage this evening

would have thought it a breeze
to spin straw into gold
or to raise Lazarus from the dead.

As we were eating,
I couldn't help seeing
the black veins in the shrimp,
the brown edges on the camellia petals.

After we'd walked the guests to their cars,
I looked up to find the full moon's face
covered with dirty blotches.

Thankfully, for all concerned, I've loosened up quite a bit. I've come to see that most people are very grateful to be served a meal that doesn't come from a cardboard box via a microwave oven. My dinner parties are "less perfect" than they were, but I do actually enjoy them.

Fact is, though, not many people actually entertain anymore. Everyone is too busy. Except for those to a few close friends and colleagues, our ties to others seem rather loose and ephemeral. Family in this country, fragmentary as it may be, is the only enduring, reliable society we have. When it disintegrates altogether, as it too often does, there's just not much left to hold the world together:

Dismembered
For Colin and Kimi

Some acts of violence leave no corpse
just an invisible body ripped
arm and leg and head from torso,
spreading its clear blood across the sky.

Thus the end of our family—
each child flung to some far horizon:

Martin to a New England prep school.
I see him sitting in a bare schoolroom
winter light slanting
down through high windows,

his pencil clutched in a grubby hand,
cramped with effort and cold.

Out of place
among the sons of the northern elite,
he never made any close friends.
"Sylvie," he said again and again,
"I'm so alone. I'm so alone."
Anna to the coast of California.
I see her running through a high green meadow,
dotted with red flowers,
her hair whipping long and black behind her.
(Just out of sight
the meadow drops abruptly
to the rocks of the Pacific.)
After being bounced
back and forth across the country
for summer and Christmas vacations,
she developed a fear of flying.
They had to fill her with Valium
before putting her on the plane.

No Valium for me as I stood there waving
goodbye,
my inner ear hearing the muscles tear,
the flesh rip from bone.

Minus my family members,
I haunted the halls and stairwells
of my boarding school dormitory,
completely unconvinced of my existence.

We never returned to each other.
There was no place to return.

I've tried to piece together
a nest of broken twigs.
Occasionally I slip up
and call my son and daughter
by my brother's and sister's names.
And sometimes after a day of rain
when I'm driving home at sunset,
the clouds just starting to clear,
I look up to find the sky
filled with shreds of wings.
There I know in the high silver light
the angels are still screaming.

I have always liked the word "remember." It seems to imply that by thinking about past events in the right way, we can re-member them, that is, put back together things that have been torn from each other but that should be part of a larger whole.

Yet clearly it is not only divorce that fractures families but cultural conditioning and contemporary social forces beyond the control of individuals to change. My children have often accused our family of being weird because we sit down together for breakfast and dinner. Their friends get to order pizzas and graze at will from the refrigerator. My favorite moment from *Judging Amy*, one of the few TV shows I've ever watched with any regularity, occurs when the whole family—Maxine, her daughter Amy, her son Peter, her nephew Kyle, and her grandchildren— are seated around the dinner table. A quarrel ensues and escalates despite attempts by the peacemakers of the family to quell it. Kyle, the ne'er-do-well nephew, says something like, "You see—this wouldn't happen if we just ate by ourselves in front of the TV like normal families."

And yet, I've discovered to my surprise, that true family harmony is possible, even if not always and forever. My husband, two children, and I are none of us easy people. We all tend to be a little high strung, judgmental, and moody. But, miraculously, we actually enjoy each other's company most of the time; and sometimes our miniature society seems almost a perfect refuge against the outside world at its most chaotic and unfathomable. The problem is, of course, that even "normal" families eventually break up as a matter of course.

The Inner Room
For Jeffrey, Aaron, and Sarah

Undoing Christmas, we wrap
the green ball, the red bird, the gold bell
in layers of tissue paper like drifts of snow.
This January night as cold
as black water under white ice.
I hear the wind sneaking under the door and know
someday one of us will go out
and not come back.

But we've built a fire on the hearth,
where it blazes like a roaring lion
devouring the night.
I've watched it hollow a log
to make an inner room
lined with glowing feathers of orange and gold.

104

Here, I think, we could all live forever,
if we could sing together with tongues of flame,
each life an alleluia in one song.

I have been a teacher of one sort or another off and on for the last twenty years. At first I taught English part time at local colleges, but more recently I've taught at private high schools. I have also been involved in "distance learning" and have taken an online computer course. But in my experience, true learning happens only when the teacher gives of him or herself; and this can occur only from the face-to-face interaction between teacher and student. What takes place between teacher and student is almost like a chemical reaction that can occur only when both are physically present. Whereas I am somewhat cynical about political reform, I believe deeply in the transforming power of education—reform that occurs from within rather than from without.

I have dabbled in several careers, but at some point I learned that I was a teacher at heart. Nothing else really seems very much worth doing. In the early days of being an "adjunct" or teaching nomad in Wisconsin, I drove at night from my home near Sheboygan over glare ice to teach in Milwaukee and through blinding snow to teach in Green Bay. I remember thinking that I must be out of my mind to risk my life for such piddling pay under such appalling conditions. And the hubris of it all—to imagine that one can single-handedly impart knowledge to a classroom of strangers. But I keep at it anyway because it is one of the things I do best and feel best about doing.

Crossing the Monitor-Merrimac Bridge
on a January Night
For My Students in English 352

All that cold black water:
in the middle of the bridge
my heart plunges down
like a plumb line
but cannot fathom
the depths of the river.
What could I have been thinking
when I hugged my husband and children goodbye

and left my house still warm
with the smells of dinner?

Across the water
the lights of the James River Bridge
glow like a strand of pearls
around the neck of a long, dark woman.
I'm on my way to teach a class—
as if my feeble light
could illumine all this darkness,
my meager warmth dilute
this vast coldness of water and sky.

On the other side of the river
the lights of the shipyards
pierce the night like braille.
But without the blindman's wisdom
I can't tell what they say.

The story of my natal family does not have the happy
ending that, up until a few years ago, I'd always hoped it would.

My sister still lives in the Bay Area, relatively isolated from the rest of the family. My brother lives hermit like in the mountains of North Carolina, still angry at the neglect he suffered when he was young. Still, perhaps I am deluded or in denial, but I think I have made my peace with the past.

For me the old shack where we first stayed when we visited our Blue Ridge Mountain property, though it no longer exists, remains in some way my only true home. It is there under the enormous oaks that used to shade its rooms that I want my ashes spread when I die. It is there that I can hear the hidden stream sing the song that is the true story of my life.

Blue Ridge Mountain Home
For my father

Three stone steps—
all that's left of the old cabin,
two large oaks—
now the only walls,
goldenrod and jewelweed growing
on ground where there used to be floor.

When I close my eyes I can
hear children laughing
smell bacon frying
in the wet morning air.

Hidden by the hemlocks,
a small stream flows beside me
down the mountain to the river—

cold and clear—
without regret.

Going Over Jordan

I had thought my story was finished, but it isn't (is any story ever really?). The last chapter must include some account of what happened after my children left home. I have said that with their help, I was able to construct an identity that was in some way more centered and stable than the one I inherited from my natal family. So who am I now that my children are gone? So many times I've heard from others, It's hard when the first one leaves, but when the last one does, you'll feel liberated; you and your husband will have your lives back to yourselves. This may be true for some couples but not, perhaps, for those of us whose worlds have been shattered when our natal families were prematurely dispersed to the four winds. I still have separation and abandonment "issues." Of course, our developmental task at this stage is simply to let go—so easy to say, so hard to do. When the major thrust of your energies has been to nurture and protect, you're suddenly asked to step away from your child and let the world have its way with him or her.

Sarah, my daughter, always emotionally precocious, began the separation process relatively early in her teens.

Sleepover

Ten o'clock
and the sun already spilling

108

through my daughter's windows
pooling in the folds of her comforter
(the one she chose herself from a catalog —
ivory slashed with red Chinese characters).
Beneath the covers,
Sarah and her friend are curled together
warm and golden as lion cubs,
Sarah's fine dark hair
swirling into her friend's
thick, honey-blonde curls.

They will not emerge for another two hours,
but in my mind's eye I watch them
from the sad height of my years.
Below they laugh and dance
at the edge of the sea,
sand warm beneath their feet.
The seafoam seems to them
lacy as their lingerie.
the glittering water brilliant
as the gems in the cheap jewelry
they're constantly giving each other.

They can't see what I see —
how the sun flashes
off each little wave
like a knife-blade.
But it's no use calling
to them. I am too far.
And even if they heard me,
they'd only giggle and wave
before plunging into the water.

I have said that up until she was twelve or so, it was hard to
tell where my identity began and my daughter's left off. Until

then, I had helped dress her, bathe her, brush her long, fine hair. She was to me a combination of friend, sister, and even mother— my reward for the early desertion of my mother and sister, the failure of so many of my female friendships. And suddenly, it seemed, she no longer needed me; in fact, she made it quite clear that I ranked way at the bottom of the list of people she most wanted to spend time with. Of course, developmentally, this was normal, and emotionally, it was wise—because the real separation was about to come; and she was doing her level best to prepare us for it. But at the time, this is not how it felt to me:

Leavings

My daughter loves all things red —
          strawberries, raspberries, cherries,
          nail polish, lipstick, rubies, and hearts.

So how, after all the stores we've haunted,
catalogs pored over together,
can she bear to leave the room
she so carefully decorated
with its red-flowered rug,
cranberry blinds,
and plum-colored pillows?
Easily enough, it seems,
since these days,
she's always eager to be somewhere else:
Starbucks, the movies, or the beach
with friends.

She's begun to shed
her childhood things

as casually as on prom night
she shrugged off
the blood-red dress
we'd bought her at some expense
and left it in a pool
on her bedroom floor.

In a few weeks
she'll be off to college.

On the kitchen table
the tops of the strawberries
she ate
before going out for pizza
with friends
lie festive as
little green windmills
after the county fair.

Within two days of the time we took Sarah up to Virginia
Tech (five hours' drive away) to begin her freshman year, our son
Aaron moved from Norfolk to Denver, Colorado. The year before,
he had graduated from William and Mary with a degree in
German studies. He had done well in school and, after spending
a year abroad at a university in Munich, spoke flawless German.
A few weeks before he was to graduate, his father and I drove up
to Williamsburg to hear him perform in his classical guitar
ensemble in the chapel of the Wren Building (the oldest on the
William and Mary campus); what he had not told us but what
became clear after the first piece was that he was the leader of the
ensemble.   However,   none   of   his   musical   or   academic

accomplishments seemed to do him a bit of good during the following year in Norfolk when he attempted to start earning a living. As Jane Tompkins points out so eloquently in her book *A Life in School: What the Teacher Learned* (which should be required reading for all teachers), schooling as we know it often does little to acquaint us with the realities of the world or even of our own psyches; rather it tends to cut us off from both. Certainly this is what happened to Aaron.

After an unsatisfactory year of dead-end jobs and failed relationships in Norfolk, Aaron packed as much of his stuff as could fit in his little gold Toyota Corolla and headed across the country to Denver, where a few of my relatives live. The poem that follows was actually written long before he left and so proved almost prophetic. I must have known at some level that to thrive, he needed to put more distance between us.

    Pale Son Gone

Even when you lived here,
you were always a little remote.

Sometimes I go and sit
in your pale blue room—
the air always cool, like you,
the white spires of Neuschwanstein Castle
rising in front of an icy lake
among snow-covered mountains
in the poster on your wall.

Always you seemed to elude me—
the fantasy novels I never quite got,

112

your perfect German I couldn't match,
the intricate pieces you composed on your guitar
but rarely performed for us.

So now you've moved to D.C.
And what is to keep you
from going on to Chicago,
to Seattle, Tokyo, Calcutta—
and finally to a place so remote
that no one can reach you?
This must be my fault, of course.
As mothers sometimes do with sons,
I let you go too early too far.
And now with twilight deepening to dusk

it's too late to call you in
to come home.

So back to my original question: Who am I now that my children are gone? One thing is certain: You don't stop being a mother when your children leave. Motherhood remains a full-time job and a permanent occupation. Once I thought of myself as Persephone; now I identify with Demeter—mater dolorosa:

Queen of Hearts

"Off with their heads,"
calls the queen, and they fall,
heavy as sodden blossoms—
white and red.
She is waiting for her husband
to return from the Crusades,
her children from the distant kingdoms

of their exile.
Somehow the growing number
of executions
seems like small consolation.

.

In the backyard
she deadheads the peonies—
white and red,
her husband gone to work,
her children to college,
a middle-aged woman
working in her garden
alone.

The fall after Sarah left for college and Aaron for Denver, I threw myself into my new job as a high school English teacher at the large, urban school from which Sarah had just graduated. I would replace my children with 130 others—65 times as many and more needy. I was so frantically busy for the next three months I barely had time to notice that I was thoroughly miserable and depressed. It was not until I adopted two very small kittens (about six weeks), recently rescued from a feral mother cat who roamed our neighborhood, that I understood how deeply my children's departure had affected me. My husband was opposed to the idea of acquiring more cats (we already had one), and when I took them in, I wasn't sure whether I was adopting them or just fostering them; I was afraid that if I gave them real names, I'd become too attached to them, so I called them Little Brother and Little Sister, which morphed into Didi and Meimei ("little brother" and "little sister" in Chinese). Of course, the names stuck, and so did the kittens. It was not until I held one of their warm purring bodies next to my chest that I realized how great the gaping hole had been that their presence was beginning to fill. From this point on, the healing began, and I started to learn how to put myself back at the center of my life (where, maybe, it had belonged all the time).

A Woman Lovely

As I stand with my cart full of groceries—
ground beef, yogurt, apples, and toilet tissue—
I must look to the checkout lady
and the other customers
like any middle-aged woman—
my hair threaded with silver,
the flesh under my chin starting to sag,
my stomach, hips, and legs,
expanding in all directions.

They don't understand that this
is not how I look at all:
Inside this middle-aged body,
my eyes glow large and dark
as Anna Karenina's;
my glossy black hair
feathers my lovely face—
neck and waist imperially slim,
elegant legs as long
as a thoroughbred filly's.

When I was younger
I was almost beautiful—
slim with long brown hair to my waist,

but underneath my golden skin
I was rather miserable,
huddled up like a child in the cold.

In those days, I wore my body
as the rhinoceros in Kipling's story
must have worn his breadcrumb-filled skin.
No wonder I was a little edgy.

After I've loaded my groceries into the car,
I slip into the driver's seat.
Reveling in my secret loveliness,
I settle into my loosened body
as in a capacious armchair
after a long but rewarding day.

It is true that now I feel more at home in myself and in my
world than I have ever felt before. Wisdom, I think, is definitely
worth the price of age. What I also know, however, is that all
homes on this earth are temporary. Some of my older friends have
died; many of both my contemporaries and my older friends are
ailing. Soon it will be time to move on again. Recently, and purely
by chance, I happened on a large exhibit of Cezanne's paintings at
the National Gallery in D.C. He is one of my favorite artists; I've
always preferred him to the Impressionists of his day (I don't say
"other" Impressionists because he never really joined their club);
many French Impressionist paintings seem to me to be all about
surfaces, but Cezanne's go deep into the muscle and heart of his
subjects. Of course his subjects were mainly the landscapes of his
native Provence, which he painted almost obsessively over and

over again—right up until the day or so before his death. With each successive painting of the same subject—for example, Mont St. Victoire—the painting became increasingly abstract so that the latest ones seem almost to convey a picture of his own psyche rather than the landscapes themselves, or perhaps the two had over time simply become one and the same. Long before I had seen this exhibit, I had written the following poem:

Forest Path, Cezanne

After the dizzying
depths, there is
nothing left
putting the inevitable
of the other,
dirt path
growing into
blues
until
invisible
my

heights and plunging
after all
but to go on
foot in front
nothing but the brown
and the trees
deeper
and greens
I am
even to
self.

Postlude

Issa wrote his *The Year of My Life* when he was fifty-six; as I write this, I am about to turn fifty-five. Issa and I have some personality traits in common as well. In eighteenth-century Japan, haiku was not just a poetic form but a way of life. The Buddhist haiku poet was by definition a wanderer; in the words of Nobuyuki Yuasa, Issa's editor and translator, "For the Japanese poet, traveling has been from time immemorial a traditional way of life and literature—a kind of symbolic and perpetual pilgrimage." Yuasa goes on to compare Issa with the earlier and more famous haiku poet Basho:

> Though both writers may be said to conform externally to this ancient pattern of the poet, traveler, and priest, Basho's and Issa's inner relation to the idea of travel was essentially quite different. For Basho it was a discipline of renunciation—an exercise in solitude—and the loneliness of all human life. For Issa, on the contrary, the road was a link that bound him more closely to other human beings. The solitude he experienced as a traveler only served to remind him more strongly of the happy home he had left behind. And it is characteristic of him that while on the road he should constantly be seeking a friend with whom to pass the night.

Like Issa, I am incorrigibly sociable. When my husband and I plan a trip, he thinks in terms of museums to visit or parks to explore; I plan our journey around visits to aunts, cousins, and friends. When I recently rather abruptly quit my job as a public high school teacher, my first thought was not "I can get on with writing my book" but "I can meet friends for lunch again."

When my son was about twelve, I experienced one of life's little epiphanies. I was frustrated because he was not turning into the person I had envisioned him to be: preferably, an Einstein, a Gandhi, or a Horowitz. Somehow, suddenly, however, I understood that it was not my job to mold him or even teach him. Mostly, I just needed to be there for him, to keep him company

118

through the days we had together. From then on parenting became easier and my approach to others wiser. I realized that we are all fellow travelers; you might board the train car I am riding, and we might sit together for a few hours, but eventually it will be time for one of us to get off the train and go our separate way. And in the final analysis, the only thing that really matters is how we treat each other for that short time we have together—with kindness, compassion, and attention; or with hostility, indifference, and neglect. As Jack Kornfield says in his book *Path with a Heart*, before we begin our spiritual quest, we each must ask ourselves, "Have I loved well?" If the answer is yes, this is all we really need to know.

I keep reading studies that try to answer such questions as why Asian children in inner cities do better academically than their white or black counterparts or why Hispanics tend to be healthier despite their relative poverty. The findings always seem to be similar: The Asian children get help on their homework at the kitchen table from caring relatives; Hispanics live in close-knit communities and tend to spend more time together than do most other Americans. And yet everything in our culture and society seems to militate against such togetherness, such closeness. Surely, it should be obvious by now that no image on the computer or television screen, transaction with an automated teller machine, or interaction with the self-checkout scanner can begin to give people what they most need and, at bottom, most want: the sight of a human face, the sound of a human voice, the touch of a human hand.

Swimming Lesson

Every day at noon
two Japanese gentlemen come
to swim in the university pool.
Choosing adjacent lanes,
they breast stroke along together
serene as swans,
their chatter soothing as
the gentle splashing of water.

Then there are the rest of us:
counting minutes, laps, and calories,
arms slicing, feet pumping,
envisioning ourselves as slim, brisk, and fit
as each of us swims alone
through all that cold blue water.

After I had finished writing most of this memoir, I thought I might not bother to get it published in the conventional manner. It seemed like too much trouble. After all, I'm past the point of wanting or needing fame and fortune. I might, I thought, just self-publish a few copies for friends and relatives. But then I realized that this book is not just about me; if it is of any value at all, it's also about you, my readers. If I can connect with even a few of you on a deeper level, publication will be worth the effort. As I tell my students, when you have lived long enough, you will realize that, as unlikely as it seems, everything is connected. Mysterious currents run through the ground of our being; odd coincidences or instances of synchronicity attest that this is true. Maybe if we

120

dig deep enough, we will find a network of underground streams that connects us all.

And so, my fellow travelers, I am glad to have had your company for a while. I hope you feel the same.

Afterword

I finished this memoir thirteen years ago in 2006. Now, in May of 2019, I have the urge to get it out among my friends and family, if nothing else. Much has happened in thirteen years. My husband was diagnosed with brain cancer in 2010 and died of it in 2011. A year ago, I myself was diagnosed with lymphoma, for which I underwent lengthy treatment. My daughter Sarah suffered some time with PTSD following the Virginia Tech massacre in 2007 and her father's death four years later when she was only twenty-four. She was a sophomore at Virginia Tech at the time of the shooting, and though she herself was not injured, a very close friend of hers was, but what really broke her heart was her father's early death. She did succeed in getting a master's degree at the University of Pennsylvania in urban planning after that, as did my son in applied linguistics at Old Dominion University at about the same time. She went on to work in nearby cities, but he, as predicted in one of my poems, ended up teaching abroad for several years in Turkey and China, where he remains. I myself retired from teaching at Old Dominion in the spring of 2016, but the peaceful retirement I'd planned was seriously disrupted by the symptoms of my incipient cancer. However, this is not the place to fill in the details of these developments. This will have to wait for another memoir. I plan to get to work on my next one as soon as I can. Stay tuned.

www.ingramcontent.com/pod-product-compliance
Lightning Source LLC
Chambersburg PA
CBHW072126090426
42739CB00012B/3084